WILD About Minnesota Birds

A Youth's Guide to the Birds of Minnesota

by Adele Porter

Adventure Publications, Inc.
Cambridge, Minnesota

This book is dedicated to Byron, Elizabeth and Rachael. Wamlati!

Acknowledgments

Carrol Henderson, Supervisor, Minnesota DNR Nongame Wildlife Program—Thank you, Carrol for your support and sharing your time and in-depth knowledge of Minnesota's lands and birds. A special thanks for allowing us to use your photographs of the Handsaker egg collection.

Joyce Frances—Your creative support and friendship continues to be an inspiration. Thank you.

Jan Welsh, Project WILD Coordinator, Minnesota DNR, Nongame Wildlife Program—Thank you, Jan for your expert input and support.

Springboard for the Arts, St. Paul, Minnesota—Thank you for your encouragement and support.

Pat, Maria, and the teachers, co-workers and students that gave of their time and talents to review the book—Thank you.

To the many students that have been the inspiration to create the book—Thank you. The natural world carries your future. Follow your curiosity, find the answers it holds, and continue to wonder.

Roland and Anna Bernau, and Mary and Orville Telford, keepers of the land to which I owe thanks for inspiring me believe in the future of native lands.

To the children of Minnesota—may your wildest wishes come true!

Edited by Gretchen Jensen, Daniel Johnson, Anthony Hertzel and Sandy Livoti

Book and cover design, nest, exterior of bird, migration map and habitat map illustrations by Jonathan Norberg

Habitat Cafe, feather and interior of bird illustrations by Julie Martinez; range maps and bird silhouette illustrations by Anthony Hertzel; cartoon bird illustrations by Brenna Slabaugh; child's nest drawing by Joshua Johnson

Photo credits by photographer and page number:

Cover photos from Shutterstock

Egg photos: T. Gilbert Pearson, *Birds of America:* 78 Chester A. Reed, *North American Birds Eggs:* 32, 46 R. L. Ridgway, *Life Histories of North American Birds:* 50, 52, 56, 58 all other egg photos from the Handsaker Egg Collection taken by Carrol Henderson

Rick and Nora Bowers: 134 (main) **Dudley Edmondson:** 44 (female), 58 (main, female), 124, 136 **Gijsbert van Frankenhuyzen/DPA*:** 102 (in flight) **John Gerlach/DPA*:** 40 (main) **Carrol Henderson:** 62 (mixed boreal forest), 90 (female), 148 (winter), 160 (in flight), 174 (gosling) **Maslowski Productions:** 78 (female) **Adele Porter:** 108 (Canada anemone) **Johann Schumacher/CLO*:** 154 (female) **Shutterstock:** 3, 6 (Black-capped Chickadee, Cooper's Hawk, Great Gray Owl), 7 (Red-tailed Hawk, Downy Woodpecker, Bald Eagle), 8 (American Pelican), 10 (Mallard, Northern Cardinal), 12, 14 (using binoculars), 15, 19, 21 (all), 24-29 (background image), 26 (coniferous forest), 27 (family fun), 60-65 (background image), 63 (both), 106-111 (background image), 140-145 (background image), 142 (Great Egret), 143 (both), 162, 186, 198 **Brian E. Small:** 68 (female), 166 (juvenile, winter) **Alan Stankevitz:** 22 (main), 30 (male), 56 (main), 58 (lift-off), 66 (main), 74 (female), 80 (main), 112 (main), 120 (horns), 130 (main), 164 (main), 180 (in flight), 182 (in flight), 184 (dinner) **Stan Tekiela:** 6 (Trumpeter Swans, Eastern Bluebird), 7 (Mallard, Indigo Bunting), 13 (American Kestrel), 14 (American Bittern), 22 (male and female), 30 (main, female), 36 (main), 38 (both), 40 (female), 42 (both), 44 (main), 46 (both), 48 (both), 50, 52 (female), 54 (all), 56 (listening for prey, in flight), 68 (main, male), 70, 74 (main), 76 (both), 78 (main), 80 (male and female, female), 82 (both), 84 (both), 86 (all), 88 (both), 90 (main), 92, 94 (side profile), 98 (all), 100 (main), 102 (main), 104 (all), 109 (American Goldfinch in winter), 112 (male winter, female), 114, 116, 118 (both), 122 (both), 124 (both), 126, 128, 130 (nesting, injury-feigning display), 132 (both), 136 (main, bottom inset), 138 (both), 142 (Bald Eagle), 146, 148 (main), 150 (both), 152 (both), 156 (all), 158 (both), 160 (main, female), 162 (female), 164 (female), 166 (main), 168 (all), 170, 172, 174 (main, in flight), 176 (all), 178 (both), 180 (main, aigrettes), 182 (main), 184 (main, in flight) **Brian K. Wheeler:** 96 (soaring), 134 (female) **Windigo:** 52 (main) **Jim Zipp:** 7 (hawk's tail), 32 (both), 34 (both), 36 (inset), 72 (both), 94 (main), 96 (main, juvenile), 100 (landing), 120 (main), 134 (wheeling), 154 (main)

*DPA: Dembinsky Photo Associates; CLO: Cornell Laboratory of Ornithology

MINNESOTA BIRDS

Thundering birds. Booming birds. Drumming birds.
Stompin', whistlin' and jazzin' birds.

Wildlife is waiting for you in Minnesota's big neighborhood of forests, prairies and wetlands. Put on your boots, grab a friend and head out the door. It's time to get WILD About Minnesota Birds!

How to Use Your Book

Wild About Minnesota Birds makes it easy to learn fascinating facts about 69 species of birds. You'll find identification tips and information on each species' favorite foods, interesting behaviors, songs and calls, life cycle, migration patterns and more.

The book is organized by habitat—the type of natural environment the bird calls home. It is divided into four sections, one for each of Minnesota's four major habitats: coniferous forests, deciduous forests, prairies and wetlands. Within each habitat section, you'll find the birds that live there arranged by size—smallest to largest—according to their length and wingspan.

For a list of the species in this book and the pages on which they appear, turn to the Table of Contents (pages 4-5). The Index (page 199) provides a handy reference guide to the species in alphabetical order. A taxonomic listing (scientific classification) of the birds is on page 198.

About Birds The beginning of this book shows the amazing characteristics that make birds unique. It explains how each part of a bird is designed to help it survive. You will also find clues to what is wild, what is a nongame bird and what is a game bird species.

How to Watch Birds Starting on page 14, this section gives you detective skills to find birds while being respectful to wildlife and the home we both share—Minnesota!

When to Watch Birds When are the best times and seasons to spy on different birds? This section, starting on page 16, helps you understand why some birds can be seen at certain times of the day or year and not others.

Where to Watch Birds Turn to page 20 to learn about our state's major land regions, and tips on where to find birds in each one.

Table of Contents

Watch for these friends!

Birding Tip

Great ideas for
bird watching fun.

Did You Know?

Gee-whiz facts that'll
WOW the whole family.

Do the Math

Brain-teasing bird math.
(Don't tell, but the answers are
on pages 194-195.)

Gross Factor

Disgusting but interesting
facts guaranteed to make
your parents gag.

History Hangout

Cool details from the past
such as where a bird's
name comes from.

Unsolved Mystery

Puzzles and oddities that have left
scientists baffled—maybe you'll
discover the solutions.

About Birds

Chickadees, Swans and Hawks. What Makes Us Birds?

Black-capped Chickadee

Trumpeter Swans

Cooper's Hawk

Feathers Birds are the only living creatures that grow feathers. They have six basic kinds. Each one helps the bird with a special job: flight, warmth, protection, balance or flotation. The color and pattern of a bird's feathers can also help you identify which species you are watching. Learn more about feathers on page 10.

Ears Yes, birds have ears under their cheek feathers. Some owls and hawks have amazing ears. Feathers arranged in a disk around the bird's face funnel sounds to its ears, helping it hear better.

Great Gray Owl

Lungs with air sacs Birds are equipped with two lungs with special balloon-like air sacs that can spread out into other parts of their bodies. This extra capacity allows a bird to store more air, push air through the lungs better and send more oxygen to its cells. This is important during long migration flights.

Eastern Bluebird

Bones Most birds have strong, flexible skeletons of hollow or semi-hollow bones with many air spaces. This helps them weigh less and—you guessed it—means lighter baggage for flying. For birds that spend a lot of time in the air, this is very important.

Oil Gland To help it stay dry in wet conditions, a bird spreads oil on its feathers. It gets the oil from the uropygium gland above its rump. The bird rubs oil on its beak, then spreads the oil over its feathers. Instant waterproofing! Ornithologists call this "preening."

Feet Most birds have four toes. Not all, though. Killdeer have just three toes, and all three face forward so the Killdeer can run fast! How the toes are arranged, such as three toes in front and one in the back, or two toes in front and two in the back, can tell you where the bird lives and how it gets around. You can get more clues about how and where the bird lives by looking at its feet. Are the feet webbed? Do they have large talons (claws)? Some birds have special toes that help them walk upside down, or hang onto a tree while pecking out a hole.

Red-tailed Hawk

Hawk's tail

Downy Woodpecker

Tail How does a bird steer or put on the brakes while flying? By spreading out its tail and adjusting its wing feathers! Each bird species has a tail designed to help it survive. A woodpecker's tail is stiff and pointed. This helps it brace itself against tree trunks while looking for food.

Songs and Calls Birds do not have vocal chords. They have a special voice box called a syrinx. They inflate air sacs to put pressure on the muscles of the syrinx, which make a range of different sounds. Nearly all birds have some sort of call, but not all birds sing. *Calls* are short and used to signal danger, warn other birds to stay away or announce mealtime. They often sound the same from one species to another. Different bird species can use and understand the same calls. *Songs* are sung mostly by males and used to attract a mate or defend their territory. These songs are complex and are only understood by birds of the same species. Try doing what birds do: sing more than one note at a time, each note at a different intensity and compose 1,000 different phrases! Wow!

Mallard

Bald Eagle

Wings Flying, diving, swooping, hovering, escaping a predator, even landing...a bird depends on its wings, which are powered by large, strong muscles anchored to the breast bone. The shape of a bird's wings can tell you a lot about where it lives, what it eats and how it catches its prey. For example, pointed wings indicate a fast flier. Large, broad wings are common among big soaring birds, while birds that maneuver around trees in a forest have short, broad wings.

Crop and Gizzard How does a bird chew food without teeth? For some birds, the food first goes into a sack called a crop, which is located near the esophagus. From there, it is sent into a two-part stomach, where the gizzard grinds it up into smaller pieces. Some birds eat gravel or eggshells (substitute teeth) that stay in their gizzards for grinding hard-to-digest food.

Beak The shape and length of a bird's beak are clues to what and how it eats. How different can beaks be? Spoon, fork, knife, straw, strainer, fish net, tweezers, pliers, nutcracker, saw and chopsticks are a few different styles. Hungry? Select your dinnerware!

American White Pelican

Anatomy

It's easier to identify birds and talk about their characteristics if you know the names of their different parts. The following illustrations point out the basic parts. Because they are composites of many species, they shouldn't be confused with any actual bird.

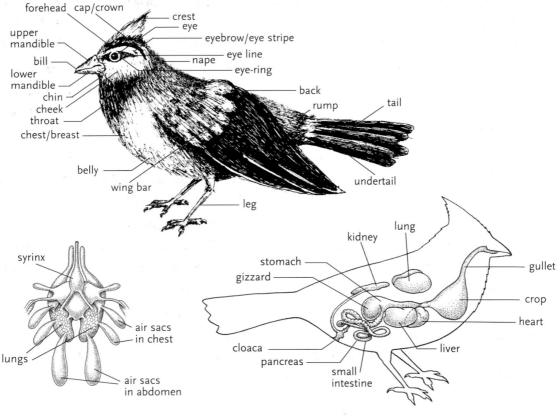

Eggs

Unlike Minnesota mammal mothers, which give birth to squirming, squalling babies, female birds lay eggs. The shell is made of calcium (the same thing bones are made of) and protects the young bird developing inside it. The shape of the egg makes for a strong shell. It is sturdy enough for parent birds to sit on and incubate (keep warm), yet fragile enough for baby birds to break through at hatching. Some birds lay colorful eggs. The colors can hide the egg from predators or help parents identify imposters.

Almost all parent birds develop a "brood patch" on their chest or belly when incubating their eggs. The feathers either fall off or are plucked out. Blood vessels next to this bare spot help keep the eggs warm. Inside the egg, the yolk is the baby bird's main source of food. The egg white provides water and protein. This food, together with a temporary egg tooth, helps the chick free itself from the shell.

Robin eggs

Nests

Bird nests are amazing. Imagine building your house strong enough to survive a storm, large enough for your growing family, insulated—and waterproof. Now, imagine finding all the materials from the natural habitat where you live. Birds do!

Just as there are different kinds of birds, there are different types of nests. Some bird species, including the Killdeer and Horned Lark, prefer a simple **ground nest** scraped out of the earth. Birds with such nests may have eggs designed to spin in place rather than roll away.

To build a nest that floats on water or balances on a cliff or bridge takes some fancy work. A **platform nest** may be built of small twigs and branches that form a simple base, with a dip in the middle to nestle the eggs. Our state bird, the Common Loon, builds its nest at the edge of a lake on a floating platform mat of reeds and mud.

Cup nests are used by most songbirds. They have a solid base attached to a tree, shrub or rock ledge. Sturdy sides are made by weaving grasses, twigs, bark or leaves tightly together. A soft, inner lining of feathers, fur or plant material keeps the eggs and young birds cozy.

Keeping a nest safe from predators calls for hanging out at the edge. A **pendulous nest** looks like a sock hanging at the end of a tree branch. It takes nearly a week for Baltimore Orioles and Ruby-crowned Kinglets to weave together the fibers of their strong watertight nests. They are such good tailors it even feels like a soft sock!

Cavity nests are used by Pileated Woodpeckers, Eastern Bluebirds and many other woodland birds. Usually chipped into a tree trunk or branch, cavity nests often have a small entrance hole that leads to an inner room. A Belted Kingfisher builds its cavity nest into a cliff or riverbank, with a long tunnel leading to the nursery.

ground nest   platform nest   cup nest   Pendulous nest   cavity nest

Feathers

When dinosaurs roamed the Earth there also lived a prehistoric, crow-sized animal with feathers; scientists believe it was related to reptiles, and have named it *Archaeopteryx* (ar kay op tehr icks) from its fossil remains. Archaeopteryx was one of the first known bird species.

Today, birds still have characteristics of their distant relatives. Reptiles have scales of solid keratin. Bird feathers are also formed of keratin, but in strands, which are much lighter. Birds are the only animals on Earth with feathers!

Mallard

Feathers help a bird fly, stay warm and dry, and protect their skin. Feathers allow birds to swim through the water and fly through the air with less friction (which makes these jobs much easier). For some birds, such as owls, feathers also quiet the sound of their flight. Feathers can be camouflage, to help them hide from predators, or bright colors to show off during courtship. Whew—feathers do a lot of things for birds!

What do birds do when their feathers start to get old? They molt (or shed) the old ones and replace them with new feathers one or two times each year. To keep their balance in flight, the feathers are shed a few at a time, in the same place on each side of the body.

Northern Cardinal

Have you noticed the "goose bumps" on the skin of a chicken from the grocery store? The bumps, called papillae, are where feathers grow out of the skin. At the bottom of each of the papillae are ligaments (similar to muscles) that the bird uses to move each feather on its own. An important function when it needs to turn in flight or slow down!

Did You Know? Have you ever heard the phrase "like water off a duck's back?" Water slides right off a duck's back because its contour feathers act like a tightly woven jacket. A duck also uses its bill to spread oil from the uropygium gland over its feathers and feet, giving them a waterproof coating.

CONTOUR FEATHERS

Contour feathers overlap each other to give birds a streamlined body shape (a contour) for less friction for faster flight in the air and faster diving in the water. Contour feathers are found on the body, wings and tail. Contour feathers have a central shaft (rachis) with vanes on each side. Attached to the vanes are barbs. On each side of the barbs are small barbules that make a "zipper" to hold the feather barbs together. When the barbs unzip, the bird uses its beak to zip them back together while preening.

DOWN FEATHERS

Down feathers do not "zip" together like contour feathers, but stay fluffy. The air spaces hold the bird's body heat close like a warm blanket. Young birds often have down first, to keep their small bodies warm until their contour and other body feathers grow in. Adult birds' down feathers are located under their contour feathers.

SEMIPLUME FEATHERS

Semiplume feathers, which are found beneath the contour feathers, are a cross between a contour and a down feather. They have a stiff shaft, but also have soft down veins that act like extra insulation.

FILOPLUME FEATHERS

Filoplume feathers are tiny, hair-like feathers comprised of a long central shaft tipped with a tuft of barbules. They help a bird adjust the position of its flight feathers. These sensitive feathers move with the slightest breeze, sending information to the nerve cells at their bases. Vibrations from the filoplume feathers tell the bird when to adjust its contour feathers for better flight.

BRISTLE FEATHERS

Bristle feathers are stiff, hair-like feathers with a firm central shaft. They are found near the eyes, nostrils and beak, and may help protect the bird's eyes, help it to locate food, and funnel prey (such as flying insects) into its mouth.

POWDER DOWN FEATHERS

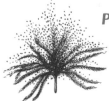

Powder down feathers, found on birds such as Great Blue Herons (pg. 182) and Great Egrets (pg. 180), are never shed, but grow all the time. The ends break down into a waxy powder that protects the bird's skin from moisture and damage.

What is Wild?

Is your pet parakeet wild? He may act wild at times, but pets and farm animals are not wild. They are domesticated animals that depend on people for survival. Wild birds find their own food, water, shelter and a place to nest and raise their young.

No one person owns wild birds. They belong to all of us. In Minnesota, wildlife biologists and managers study wild birds and their habitats. The information is used to make laws that protect wildlife and wild places. Conservation officers make sure everyone follows these rules, and you can help! If you see someone breaking the law, ask an adult to call the Turn In Poachers tip line, (800) 652-9093. They can remain anonymous and may even get a cash reward. Together, we can make sure Minnesota birds are around for a long time.

Leave Wild Things Wild

Wild birds and animals were once considered unlimited resources. They were killed for meat, feathers and hides without seasons or limits. By the late 1800s, unregulated market hunting (along with habitat destruction) caused many species—from the American Bison to Great Egret—to almost disappear forever. The Passenger Pigeon, which once darkened the skies with its huge flocks, eventually did become extinct.

Fortunately, a series of laws including the Lacey Act and Migratory Bird Treaty Act helped protect other wild birds before it was too late. These laws governed the harvest of migratory birds, including their eggs, nests and feathers. Today, many state and federal laws protect wild birds, animals and the habitats they need to survive.

Great Egret

The eggs shown in the species accounts of this book are from a famous collection of wild bird eggs gathered by Iowa farmer Ralph Handsaker in the late 1800s and early 1900s. Although wild bird eggs are now protected, in that era, collecting eggs was a popular hobby for naturalists. Handsaker's collection consisted of nearly 4,000 eggs from around the world and more than 400 species of birds. It is the focal point of the book *Oology and Ralph's Talking Eggs* by wildlife biologist Carrol Henderson. The collection is now at the Peabody Museum of Natural History at Yale University.

It's tempting to enjoy nature by taking part of it home with us. But it is important to keep wild things wild, and leave eggs, nests and baby birds alone.

Game or Nongame Wildlife?

Ring-necked Pheasant

Wildlife that can be hunted under Minnesota law, such as the Ring-necked Pheasant, is called **game wildlife**. The Minnesota Department of Natural Resources (DNR) regulates hunting so it does not threaten game bird populations. For their part, hunters buy licenses and stamps, and pay special taxes on hunting gear; this raises millions of dollars for habitat protection and management that benefits all wildlife.

Birds that are not legally hunted are considered **nongame wildlife**. This book is mostly about nongame birds.

The DNR's Nongame Wildlife Program keeps a special eye on more than 500 species of birds, animals, reptiles and amphibians in Minnesota. Donations to the Nongame Wildlife Fund, mainly through a special checkoff on state income tax forms, help the program conduct important research, habitat protection and other management efforts. Ask your parents to look for the "Line with the Loon" on Minnesota tax forms. Citizens can also donate to the Nongame Wildlife Program on the DNR website: www.dnr.state.mn.us.

What's in a Name? *Binomial Nomenclature*

Some people call this bird a kestrel; some a sparrow hawk; and still others call it a killy hawk after its call, "killy, killy, killy." So, which is right? In Minnesota, the official common name of this small falcon is American Kestrel. But a species' common name can be different from place to place; especially if the people speak a different language.

Scientists saw the problem with common names and decided that each living thing needed a name that was exactly the same all over the world. They developed a system of scientific names called **binomial nomenclature** (by-no-me-all no-men-clay-chur).

American Kestrel

Whether you're in Minneapolis or Madagascar, a bird's scientific name is always in the same language: Latin. Scientific names are written in italic, or *slanted* letters. Each scientific name has two words. The first is always capitalized and is the genus, meaning the big group it belongs in. The second word is not capitalized and is the species. The American Kestrel's scientific name is *Falco sparverius*. Knowing this, you're well on your way to becoming a real scientist.

13

How to Watch Birds

We live in a big neighborhood! In Minnesota, we share our land with wildlife neighbors that depend on us to treat them with respect and care. Here are some tips for successful wildlife watching and being a responsible next-door neighbor to wildlife.

To Find One, Be One!

Your best chance of spying on wildlife is by thinking like a bird.

American Bittern

MOVE SLOWLY AND BLEND IN

Sudden movements may startle wildlife. So make like a snail. Or better yet, take a lesson from the American Bittern, a bird found around shallow wetlands and lake edges. The bittern eats small prey such as crayfish, frogs and fish. It catches them by S-L-O-W-L-Y stalking along shorelines. The bittern's best moves are almost as slow as the hour hand on a clock. Bitterns also stand still, watching, until dinner swims a little too close . . . gotcha!

You don't have to catch your food, but moving slowly can help you see more birds. So can blending in. The bittern knows this, too. Its grass-colored feathers are a great disguise. Because part of being a successful wildlife detective is working unnoticed, it's smart to wear drab-colored clothing. Camouflage patterns that match your surroundings work great. Birds will be less likely to see you, and you may get a better look at them!

SHHH...BE QUIET, LIKE AN OWL IN FLIGHT

Some birds have very good ears. If you talk and make noise, they will hear you coming long before you see them. Great Horned Owls are super hunters partly because they keep quiet. Special feathers help them silently swoop down on mice and other small animals. When you're spying on birds, think like an owl and don't make a sound! Some birds also use their feet to feel the vibrations of your footsteps. So walk lightly if you want to spy a bird before it flies away with the wind.

KEEP YOUR DISTANCE

If you saw a giant watching you, would your legs feel shaky? Wildlife can feel like this if you get too close. Binoculars and spotting scopes can give you a close-up view from far away. If you're not using binoculars, don't turn your head to look at something to the side. Try moving only your eyes. Animals do this to spy on YOU!

Using binoculars

LISTEN UP!

Bird calls, songs and other sounds can be hard to hear, especially at a distance. To improve your hearing, cup your hands behind your ears. It's amazing what you can hear now!

Wing marks on the snow

If you don't see any birds right away, look for signs they've been in the neighborhood. These include clues such as wood chips scattered around the base of a tree, holes pecked in a soft or decayed tree, droppings, food scraps and empty seed shells, wing marks on the snow, even a stray feather.

FEEDING TIPS

It's fun to feed birds in your backyard, but don't try it in the big neighborhood that includes prairies, parks, forests and shores. Check the **Today's Special** listing for each species to find out what each bird likes to eat; some include tips on what to put in your backyard feeders.

Snap Photos Safely

Wild birds and animals can be unpredictable. They sometimes move fast, often without you knowing ahead of time. So keep a safe distance. Many cameras have a zoom lens that allows you to get close-up photos, while staying a safe distance away.

You may need to remind the adults with you about this safety tip. If your mom or dad thinks it would be cute to have a photo of you standing next to a Moose or Canada Goose, tell them to use the zoom lens and leave you out of the picture.

Souvenir Shopping

Souvenirs help us remember fun times. A photograph, drawing, artwork and your own stories are super souvenirs of time afield. Leave everything else in the outdoor neighborhood— including baby animals that look like they're all alone. Resist the temptation to "rescue" them. Chances are, the mother is nearby.

Look But Don't Touch

Your pet hamster may enjoy being picked up, but wild animals do not. Don't try to pet or touch a wild bird or animal; it will get scared and may bite, peck or scratch you. Keep your distance, especially during nesting season.

If you really want to give wildlife a "hug," build a birdhouse or backyard feeder. Leave our big Minnesota neighborhood the way it was when you found it. Then give yourself a pat on the back for being a responsible wildlife neighbor.

When to Watch Birds

Day, night, summer, winter. **When is the best time to spy on birds?**
Look for the **clues**.

Birds Move When they are the least likely to be seen and caught by a predator; their food is available; they need the most energy and refueling; and when they need to, according to the changing seasons.

DAYTIME = DIURNAL

Birds that are active in the day and sleep at night are called diurnal. Why daytime? Think like the bird. For example, hummingbirds are active in the day because the flowers that hold the nectar they need only open in sunlight.

TWILIGHT = CREPUSCULAR

Many animals can be best watched at dawn (when the sun is just coming up) and at dusk (when the sun is going down). Why dawn and dusk? There is enough light for the animals to see where they need to go, but not enough for some predators to hunt them. At twilight they appear like faint shadows.

NIGHTTIME = NOCTURNAL

Birds that are active at night and sleep during the day are called nocturnal. These animals have special adaptations for being up all night. Owls have excellent hearing and special nighttime and daytime vision.

Journaling and Phenology

Phenology is the study of the seasonal changes and movements of nature. The return of the first robin in spring; the migration of monarch butterflies; the first and last snow of the year; and the first ground squirrel you spy after winter hibernation, are all part of Minnesota phenology. Wildlife biologists and ornithologists use phenology records to help them understand the needs and behaviors of birds.

You can be a part of Minnesota's ongoing wildlife studies by keeping a journal. It's as simple as writing in a notebook or on a calendar. Get started with the journal section beginning on page 186. Journals are fun to look back on. Plus, your addition to Minnesota's record might one day help scientific research!

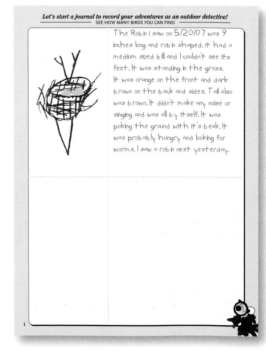

Let's start a journal to record your adventures as an outdoor detective!
SEE HOW MANY BIRDS YOU CAN FIND

The Robin i saw on 5/20/07 was 9 inches long and robin shaped. It had a medium sized bill and I couldn't see its feet. It was standing in the grass. It was orange on the front and dark brown on the back and sides. Tail also was brown. It didn't make any noise or singing and was all by itself. It was poking the ground with it's beak. It was probably hungry and looking for worms. I saw a robin nest yesterday.

Women in Science Almira Torgerson (1893–1928) of Fosston explored the oak savanna-parkland region of northwestern Minnesota after school. Keeping journals of the birds she saw may not have seemed like a big deal to her at the time, but today she is recognized as an important woman in science. Almira taught in Polk County schools during the day and explored the wilds of northern Minnesota during her time off. Her migration records and other notes were used by the Minnesota Game and Fish Department (today called the Minnesota Department of Natural Resources) and the U.S. Biological Survey in Washington, D.C. to establish a scientific record and population status of many northern bird species. No doubt her students had a fascinating teacher!

Seasons

Understanding how the changing seasons affect Minnesota's birds will bring you wildlife watching success.

SPRING

Once the ice leaves the lakes, usually in mid-March, listen and watch overhead for returning birds. Look for waterfowl, hawks and blackbirds to lead the way. Shorebirds arrive in May. Warblers arrive in mid- to late May.

Birds are busy in the spring, finding a date and a mate. This is when males defend their territory, sing and do all kinds of tricks to attract a female or two. It's a very entertaining time of year!

SUMMER

Summer Gross Factor On hot summer days, some birds excrete waste down their legs to help cool themselves through evaporation. Gross, but cool!

In summer, birds are busy breeding (mating), nesting and raising their young. Shhh...by mid-July it quiets down. In some species, males leave the nesting area in late July or early August for a quiet place where they molt (shed) their bright breeding feathers and grow in duller colored plumage. They are ready for flight in time for migration.

FALL

By August, Canadian birds begin to pass through on their migration south. They are joined by some Minnesota birds. Many species begin to group up in large migratory flocks and feed heavily in preparation for migration.

In Minnesota, winter means cold. Birds that stick around have slick strategies for dealing with the cold, snow and changes in food supply.

To beat the cold, birds grow an extra layer of feathers for the winter, like putting on a winter coat. Some will also fluff out their feathers to create more air pockets, which trap heat close to their bodies. Others lower their body temperatures at night to reduce the amount of energy (and therefore food) needed to keep warm.

Another strategy is to make a group huddle—there's warmth in numbers! And some birds sit on their legs, or tuck a leg and foot, one at a time, into their warm body feathers.

How do the tiny legs of chickadees keep from freezing in the winter? Instead of having their veins and arteries separated by muscle like we do, theirs are side by side in their legs. The warm blood coming from their heart is right next to the cool blood flowing back to it from their legs. Heat exchanges between them!

Speaking of legs, some birds grow extra feathers around their legs and feet, or extra scales on the outside edge of their feet, for use as snowshoes to stay on top of deep snow!

Because food supplies often run low in winter, some bird species store food in bark cracks, crevices and tree cavities. Others bulk up (gain fat) in the fall in preparation for the extra energy demands of winter.

Because there is less competition for nest sites and food, some hardy birds may take advantage of the situation and begin nesting in winter.

Migration

Boreal migrants live in Canada but come south into Minnesota when their northern food supply is short.

Permanent residents are birds that stick it out and stay in Minnesota all year.

Short-distance migrants go just far enough south to avoid the extreme temperatures of our Minnesota winters and return to breed in the spring. They travel to wintering grounds located from Iowa to Texas and Florida.

Mid-distance migrants breed in (or north of) Minnesota and migrate to wintering areas in Central America.

Long-distance migrants breed here, but migrate to wintering areas in South America. These migrants travel up to 7,000 miles on their way from Minnesota to their wintering grounds.

Key

- ■ **Boreal Migrants**
- ■ **Permanent Residents**
- ■ **Short-distance Migrants**
- ■ **Mid-distance Migrants**
- ■ **Long-distance Migrants**

Where to Watch Birds

Make bird identification easy on yourself. Narrow down the possibilities by first knowing the habitat. After all, it is of little use looking for a water bird like a Common Loon on a prairie, or a prairie bird like the Burrowing Owl on a lake!

Minnesota Habitats

Have you noticed that some wild places look different than others? Some have few trees and a lot of grass; others are covered with trees; and some are a mixture of trees, shrubs and grass. That's because Minnesota has different types of ecological systems, or habitats, and there are many different kinds of trees, shrubs and grasses within these habitats.

FANTASTIC FOUR

Minnesota has four main kinds of habitats: coniferous forests, deciduous forests, prairies and wetlands. In each of these habitats, a combination of the climate (weather and seasons), geography, land history and soil support different kinds of wild plants, birds and animals. In a northern coniferous forest, you can spy on Spruce Grouse "in the house" and Moose on the loose. On a western prairie, you're more likely to see Bobolinks bobbin' and Greater Prairie-Chickens boomin'.

Minnesota has three major land regions. The area highlighted in green once supported primarily coniferous trees. Deciduous (red) and prairie (yellow) were the dominant habitats in the other two regions. Wetlands are found throughout the state.

The forests and prairie habitats once closely followed the land regions on the map at left (wetlands were found statewide). Because people have replanted the landscape for various purposes, we now have a mixture of habitats across the state. However, the original land regions are still a good guide to the dominant native habitat in each area.

To match these habitats, *Wild About Minnesota Birds* is divided into four main sections: Coniferous Forest; Deciduous Forest; Prairie and Open Grasslands; and Wetlands, Rivers, Lakes and Shores. The 69 birds in this book appear in the habitat section where you are most likely to see them. Of course, many can live in more than one habitat. And some birds are able to live almost anywhere. We have called these species *"Super Adaptors."* Can you find birds in all four of Minnesota's major habitats? **Go for it!**

HIGHS AND LOWS

Most birds are more often found—or easier to see—at different levels in their habitat. For example, you're more likely to see a Wild Turkey strutting across the forest floor than soaring through the air. But just the opposite is true if you're looking for a Purple Martin. To help you know where to look, a large picture at the beginning of each section shows the habitat. Silhouettes of each bird species are placed within it where you're most likely to see them, particularly during the day.

The silhouettes don't always indicate where a bird spends most of its time. Some show where the bird is easiest to see. Ring-necked Pheasants can be tough to spot when they are on the ground, tucked in grasses and other hiding cover. But they're hard to miss when they fly to escape a predator, or to hustle from a feeding area to their evening roost.

Coniferous Forest

Deciduous Forest

Prairie, Open Grasslands and Fields

Wetlands, Rivers, Lakes and Shores

Common Name

Scientific Name

Length: Size of bird from tip of bill to tip of tail
Wingspan: Measurement from wing tip to
wing tip with wings outstretched

male and female

female

FIELD MARKS are the unique characteristics that make one bird species different from another. These include its color, feather pattern, bill, wings, feet and tail shape.

Look for the captions that point out field marks to help you identify the birds you watch.

Most large photos are of a male in breeding plumage (feather color and pattern).

Photos to help you identify juveniles, females or other plumage patterns; also images of interesting bird behavior (top)

Look here for information about calls, songs and other sounds the bird makes—and what they mean.

About This Bird

This section provides interesting natural history information about the featured species. This could be descriptions of its survival strategies or preferred habitat, how it looks for food, or how it attracts a mate, builds a nest and cares for its young. Look here also for bird watching manners, tips for success and fun ways to be involved in providing for the needs of birds.

80

Habitat Café

Today's Special
check this sign for interesting menu items

Yumm . . . bring an order of ants and grubs. Did you say the winter special is spider egg cases? What a bird eats, how much it needs, and when the food is available plays a BIG part in a species' behavior and survival. When you know what a bird eats in each season, you'll know when and where to spy on them.

SPRING, SUMMER, FALL, WINTER MENU:
What a bird eats by season

Life Cycle

NEST The kind of nest this bird builds to incubate its eggs and raise its young; who builds the nest; what the nest is made of and where it is located.

EGGS How many, how big or small, how long it takes to incubate the eggs and which parent does the duty of egg sitting.

MOM! DAD! The role of parent birds in early chick life. Altricial chicks are born naked, blind, unable to move around, and are totally dependent on their parents. Precocial chicks hatch complete with downy feathers and the ability to walk or swim to food that they can eat on their own. Parents provide guidance and protection.

NESTLING What goes on in the nest? Look here to find out how fast the nestlings mature.

FLEDGLING When do young birds leave the nest?

JUVENILE The final changes into adulthood mean independent flight, food gathering and preparation for migration or overwintering. Completing the life cycle means the ability to find a mate and nest!

History Hangout

Look here for more fascinating details about the species, under the headings History Hangout, Birding Tips, Do the Math, Did You Know? and Gross Factor. You'll find interesting facts, challenging math questions (the answers are provided on pages 194-195), ideas for better bird watching and fun, gross facts about birds.

When
Look to this box for clues about when the bird is active. The symbols will tell you whether the bird is active during the night (nocturnal), day (diurnal) or at twilight (crepuscular).

Migration
Does this bird migrate or stick around in the cold and snow? Knowing what a bird is doing during each season will help you know when and where to watch for it. When does it arrive in spring? When does it leave in fall? Where does it spend the winters? Look here to find out.

Nesting
Look in this section to discover when the bird starts nesting.

Getting Around
Birds have many different ways to get where they need to go. Think like the bird you are looking for. Ask, "If I am a _____, how will I get around? Flying, hopping, gliding, diving, wading, soaring?" A Hummingbird hovers and doesn't use its legs for walking. Now, that's something to think about.

Where to Look
Check the range map to see where and when to look for each bird. The notes offer tips on specific locations.

Year-round Migration	Summer Winter

Habitat Type   81

Coniferous Forest

The seeds of coniferous trees develop inside cones. Most of these trees are evergreen. Their leaves (needles) stay green and do not fall off every year. Why? Turn the pages to explore the coniferous forests of the north.

Land Before Time

Explore the northern Boundary Waters Canoe Area Wilderness and find yourself with feet planted on the exposed rock of the Canadian Shield, a layer of rock 2.5 billion years old. You are standing on ancient history from well before even the dinosaurs!

The Wisconsin Glacier brought remarkable changes to the land about 10,000 to 75,000 years ago. The actions of this powerful, mile-high sheet of ice paved the way for the coniferous forests of northeastern Minnesota.

Tough Trees

Unlike the prairie, which nurtures plants with several feet of rich earth, northern Minnesota has very shallow soils that are much lower in nutrients. The weather is also more extreme. To survive such harsh conditions, coniferous trees are well adapted to the short growing season, cold, heavy snowfall and shallow, acidic soils.

Coniferous Forest

Their shallow root systems draw nutrients from the topsoil. A wax covering on their needles protects them from the extreme cold and winter winds. The needles stay on all year. This saves energy and provides more time to turn sunlight and water into plant energy (photosynthesis). Conifers are tough, too; their branches can bend with heavy snowfall.

Coniferous trees of the northern forest include red, white and jack pine, balsam fir, white cedar, white and black spruce and tamarack. Some deciduous trees have also adapted to the conditions found here, including aspen, paper birch and in some areas, red oaks, basswood, northern pin oaks and maples.

Walk On A Huge Sponge?

You can, when you venture onto one of northern Minnesota's peat bogs. Formed in shallow basins left by retreating glacial ice, which later filled with rainwater, these bogs are in a world of their own.

The high acidity of the peat (rich organic material made up mostly of partially decayed plant material); cool year-round temperatures; and the limited oxygen supply due to poor water circulation, discourage bacteria and other decomposers from breaking down plant material. Over years the plant matter builds up, resulting in a thick, floating mat of peat.

Plants that grow in the acidic, water-logged peat have adapted to the conditions. Coniferous, cone-bearing trees of a bog include black spruce, tamarack and northern white cedar. The needles of tamaracks turn bright yellow in autumn before falling off. Because of this trait, tamaracks are a very unusual cone-bearing tree!

Be safe about bog-trotting. It's a good idea to venture onto a bog only with someone that knows the area. Public areas with boardwalks are safe, and provide easy walking. Try Sax-Zim Bog near the small towns of Sax, Zim and Kelsey in St. Louis County for a look at Great Gray Owls, Boreal Chickadees, Ruby-crowned Kinglets, Red-breasted Nuthatches, White-throated Sparrows, Ruffed Grouse, Snowy Owls and Gray Jays. People come from all over the world to get a glimpse of these amazing birds!

Winter Wonderland

You can explore the wilds of northern Minnesota in the winter, too. It's a great time to learn how the hearty birds that live there year-round survive the cold, snow and changes in their food supply. Their adaptations to the cold climate are fantastic!

Family fun

Some birds grow extra layers of feathers for insulation; others huddle together to stay warm; the Spruce Grouse even creates an igloo-like burrow in the snow! Turn to page 18 to learn more about how northern Minnesota birds survive winter.

When the snow squeaks underfoot, take a clue from the local wildlife and dress in layers, wear warm boots or snowshoes, take along water and a snack for extra energy, and buddy-up with a friend.

Look for wing marks in the snow, wood chips scattered below a tree from the local woodpecker's hole drilling, snow crystals outlining a grouse snow burrow, and follow the tracks in the snow that tell a story. Be adventurous and, of course, always be safe!

Check Off the Coniferous Birds You See!

When you spot coniferous birds, use these pages to check them off. The locations of these illustrations indicate where you might see them.

28

Ruby-throated Hummingbird

Archilochus colubris

Length: 3–3½ inches
Wingspan: 4½ inches

male

female

Females have a
white throat

Iridescent
green back

Male has ruby
red throat

Light gray-white belly
and breast

Stiff, narrow wings
rotate in their sockets.
Large muscles power
a fast figure eight
movement.

Wings make a
bumblebee-like humming
sound in flight.
Communicates with quiet
twitters and chatters

Minnesota's Smallest Bird

Small bird—big appetite. Hummingbirds have the highest energy output per unit of weight of any living warm-blooded animal. What does this mean? For such a tiny bird it uses a huge amount of energy. How does it supply this energy? It must feed every few minutes and survives the night without food by lowering its body temperature and heart rate. To invite this tiny bird to your backyard, plant tube-like flowers including bee-balm (monarda), cardinal flower, bergena and trumpet vine. Include a nectar feeder. You can make nectar by boiling one cup of white sugar with four cups of water. Change the nectar often to keep your backyard hummingbirds healthy!

Habitat Café

Yumm . . . bring an order of nectar from up to 2,000 flowers per day, with a side order of insects and spiders. Ruby-throated Hummingbirds are omnivorous. Tongue is longer than their bill, with a forked tip and grooves for the nectar to follow up the tongue like a straw.

Today's Special
sugar water from nectar feeders

SPRING, SUMMER, FALL, WINTER MENU:
Mostly nectar from flowers, with a few insects and spiders

Life Cycle

NEST The female builds the less than 2-inch cup nest on a tree twig or small coniferous branch, usually 15–25 feet above ground. She weaves plant down and bud scales to the limb with spider silk and disguises the outside with moss and lichens.

EGGS About ½ inch long. The female incubates the clutch of 2 eggs for 12–14 days.

MOM! DAD! Altricial. Mom parents the chicks, feeding them a mixture of regurgitated nectar and insects while hovering gently above.

NESTLING Chicks hear their mom's mew call and feel the air from her wing beats that signal, time for lunch!

FLEDGLING Young leave the nest when they are 18–20 days of age.

JUVENILE The teenagers become adults and are able to date, mate and raise their own young when they are 1–2 years old.

Do the Math

A hummingbird eats an average of 30 percent of its weight in nectar in one day! If you weigh 100 pounds, how many pounds of nectar would you need to eat each day? Do the math. _____ (your answer) Just before their long migration, hummingbirds double their body mass by feeding on even more nectar and insects. Double your body weight—now how many pounds of nectar would you possibly eat in one day? Do the math again. _____ Wow! Answer on pages 194-195.

When

Ruby-throated Hummingbirds are diurnal, active during the day and resting at night.

Migration

Long-distance migrant, wintering in Central America to Costa Rica. Some fly 480 miles on a 20-hour, nonstop flight across the Gulf of Mexico. On their spring return, they depend on Yellow-bellied Sapsuckers to drill holes that leak sap. This is the main menu until flowers bloom.

Nesting

Begins in late May–June in the state, mostly north and east.

Getting Around

Masters of movement, they fly backward, forward, upside down and hover in one place. They are known to fly 60 miles per hour with up to 75 wing beats per second! Hummingbirds do not walk or hop—they use their small feet only for perching.

Where to Look

Wooded areas, backyard flower plantings and nectar feeders throughout Minnesota. Areas with large flower gardens or wildflowers.
· Itasca State Pk (Douglas Lodge)

Year-round   Summer
Migration   Winter

Ruby-crowned Kinglet

Regulus calendula

Length: 3½–4 inches
Wingspan: 7–8 inches

White eye-ring

Males have a small ruby-red king's crown that is raised and seen only during spring courtship

Except for the male's red crown, females, juveniles and males look the same

Olive green above and pale gray below

Wings have two white wing bars

"Tee-da-leet, tee-da-leet, tee-da-leet."
This loud warbling song sung by males is heard over half a mile away!

Elfin Kings of the North

One of Minnesota's smallest birds, the Ruby-crowned Kinglet only nests and raises its young in northern coniferous forests. They are specialists. It is a different story when it comes time to pack their feathers for spring and fall migration. They will check into nearly any wayside hotel—coniferous, deciduous and floodplain forests, farm windbreaks, fields and backyards. This ability to adapt to different habitats during migration has helped kinglets survive the changes people have made to wild lands. August–October and again in March–May are the best times to spot kinglets as they migrate and fill up at backyard feeders. After all, 1,000 miles is a long flight for these elfin kings of the North!

Habitat Café

Today's Special
nectar from a hummingbird feeder

Yumm . . . bring an order of spiders, beetles, bugs, ants, moths and berries. Ruby-crowned Kinglets are omnivorous. They also enjoy bird feeder treats such as suet, peanuts and walnut pieces.

SPRING, SUMMER, FALL, WINTER MENU:
Lots of insects and some seeds

Life Cycle

NEST The female builds the small, deep, sock-like nest cup 2–100 feet above the ground, hidden on the end of a coniferous tree branch. She weaves twigs, plant stems, moss and lichens together with spider silk and lines it with soft fur. The nest is so narrow that eggs are laid in layers.

EGGS About ½ inch long. The female incubates the clutch of 5–11 eggs for 11–14 days. The large number of eggs and young offsets their usual life span of 2 years—although some live 5 years or more.

MOM! DAD! Altricial. Both parents feed the young regurgitated (spit up) baby formula the first few days. Diaper duty is shared.

NESTLING Mom keeps the young safe and warm by brooding them at shorter and shorter periods as they grow.

FLEDGLING The stretchy nest expands to hold the growing chicks. There is a limit, and by 12–16 days, the chicks squeeze out of the nest pouch. Parents bring insects until they are four weeks of age.

JUVENILE Ruby-crowned Kinglets are mature enough to date, mate, nest and raise their own young the following spring.

Did You Know?

Birds' bones are so light that their feathers may weigh more than all of the bones in their skeleton. This includes species that migrate long distances. In 1927, Charles Lindbergh, the first person to fly an airplane nonstop from New York to Paris, France, sat in a wicker chair and took with him only sandwiches, survival gear and two canteens of water to keep the weight low in his canvas-covered airplane. He even tore off the edges of his paper map to reduce weight. Keep it light for a fuel-efficient flight.

When
Diurnal. They feed during the day and rest at night.

Migration
Boreal migrant. In autumn, they move through Minnesota from the boreal forests of Canada. Mid- to long-distance migrant. Resident kinglets migrate in the fall to the southern U.S., Mexico and Central America to escape the cold and find a plentiful supply of food.

Nesting
Resident kinglets nest in spruce trees near a wet area like a swamp or bog during May in Minnesota.

Getting Around
Ruby-crowned Kinglets pick up insects from branches, cones and needles while they hover. They also "hawk" flying insects, snatching them in flight from the air. Nearly always in motion, they flit quickly and directly from branch to branch, jerking their wings in a nervous flight.

Where to Look
Coniferous and boreal forests of northeastern Minnesota. Most often found 15–50 feet above the ground in trees.
· Chippewa Nat'l Forest
· Cedar Creek

Year-round	Summer
Migration	Winter

Coniferous Forest Habitat

33

Brown Creeper

Certhia americana

Length: 5–5½ inches
Wingspan: 7–8 inches

hunting for insects

Whitish eyebrow above dark eye

Short legs keep the creeper close against the tree

Three front toes joined at the base for added support; long, sharp, curved claws give extra grip.

Females and males are brown with buff-white streaks, just like the tree bark they creep on. They are white below with a rusty colored rump.

Stiff, long tail feathers used as a prop

"Trees, trees, trees, see the trees." Males sing this territory song in spring and summer until the young chicks leave the hidden nest.

The Great Scavenger Hunt

The Brown Creeper scavenger hunts for insects in the cracks of tree trunks. Finding the prize is a matter of direction—it creeps UP trees headfirst. Starting at the bottom of the trunk, a Brown Creeper climbs up, sometimes spiraling around the tree like a stripe around a candy cane. When it gets close to the top, it flies to the bottom of a nearby tree to begin its hunt again. Another hunter— the nuthatch—goes DOWN trees headfirst to find insects. These different views give both species a good chance of finding insects missed by the other. This makes winners out of both players. Teamwork.

Habitat Café

Today's Special
peanut butter and suet
BIRD FEEDER TREAT

Yumm . . . bring an order of ants, caterpillars, insect eggs and larvae, moths, beetles and spiders. Brown Creepers are insectivores. Their long, thin, down-curved bill gleans (picks up) insects from tree bark cracks.

SPRING, SUMMER, FALL MENU:
Mostly insects, some seeds

WINTER MENU:
More seeds than summer, but still mostly insects

Life Cycle

NEST With spider webs, the female attaches twigs, leaves and shreds of bark to make a hammock-like nest behind a loose piece of bark on the side of a dead or dying tree. The inner nest cup is lined with fine bark shreds and moss to keep the eggs and chicks warm.

EGGS Slightly longer than ½ inch. The female incubates the clutch of 5–6 eggs for 14–15 days.

MOM! DAD! Altricial. Mom broods the chicks for the first 10 days. Both parents feed the chicks and do their part in chick diaper duty from the time the chicks hatch until they are 5–6 weeks of age.

NESTLING Bad hair day! The chicks are born with a very funny hairstyle. They have absolutely no feathers except for some gray down arranged in rows just above both their eyes!

FLEDGLING They leave the nest at age 17–18 days. At night the young come together in a circle, with heads facing inward and the feathers on their necks and shoulders fluffed out.

JUVENILE At one year old, the birds are mature enough to date, mate, nest and raise their own young.

Birding Tip

Take a trip to one of Minnesota's nature centers and wild outdoor areas to look for Brown Creepers. Lowry Nature Center, Wood Lake Nature Center, Itasca State Park and the state parks along Lake Superior's North Shore all provide habitat for this small northern insect-eater. Pack your wildlife watching manners and plan for fun!

When
Diurnal. They feed during the day and rest at night.

Migration
Permanent resident to short-distance migrant, with some overwintering in Minnesota. In September and October, they move to deciduous and wooded areas in towns and parks in southeastern parts of the state. Others may migrate as far south as Illinois.

Nesting
Brown Creepers return to the northern coniferous forests in late March and early April. They nest in April–May.

Getting Around
Parent creepers teach their young to act like a leaf and flatten out when danger is near. They make short flights from tree to tree when feeding. In keeping with their spiral pattern of foraging up a tree, the male and female fly around a tree when they are doing their dating and mating dance.

Where to Look
Mature, old growth coniferous and mixed coniferous-deciduous forests, and timbered swamps with dead or dying nesting trees.
· Itasca State Pk
· Lowry Nature Ctr
· Wood Lake Nature Ctr

Year-round Migration	Summer Winter

Boreal Chickadee

Poecile hudsonica

Length: 5–5½ inches
Wingspan: 8 inches

Brown cap
and back

Color varies from grayish
brown to brownish gray

Females and males
look the same

Rusty colored sides

"Pst-zee-zee-zee!" This soft song is sung up to 60 times per hour. When incubation starts, it drops to only 30.

Hide and Seek, Chickadee-style

Cold, it is very cold in northern Minnesota in the winter. The weather changes often. To survive in the North Woods, Boreal Chickadees have become champion adaptors. For these tiny birds, having enough fuel to keep warm is a matter of hide and seek. Chickadees hide seeds and insects in the cracks of tree bark, branches and under tree needles in later summer and fall and then seek them when the weather is too cold or snowy for hunting. Before nightfall, they can gain 10 percent of their weight in body fat. They use this fatty fuel overnight and rebuild it again the next day. On a winter night, their body temperature drops as much as 20 degrees, using far less fuel to stay warm.

Habitat Café

Yumm . . . bring an order of caterpillars, wasps, bees, ants, beetles, bugs, spiders and tree seeds—hemlock, fir, pine and spruce. Boreal Chickadees are omnivorous. Chickadees use spit, spider web silk or insect cocoon silk to hold a seed or insect in a hiding place.

Today's Special
peanut butter and suet
BIRD FEEDER TREAT

SPRING, SUMMER, FALL MENU:
Lots of insects, some seeds

WINTER MENU:
Equal amounts of insects and seeds

Life Cycle

NEST The nest hole is made by another animal or made new by chickadees in the soft, rotten wood of a tree trunk. The female does most of the work, hammering wood chips loose and tossing or carrying them out. The nest hole is lined with moss and animal fur.

EGGS About ½ inch long. The female incubates the clutch of 6–7 eggs for 12–15 days. She eats the egg shells once the chicks have hatched. Yum, calcium.

MOM! DAD! Altricial. Both parents feed the newly hatched, blind and naked chicks. Delivering over 20 meals per hour can keep a parent bird very busy. For each meal there is a fecal sac (diaper) to carry away.

NESTLING The chicks grow white down and then full feathers.

FLEDGLING At 18 days of age, they leave the nest and within the next week, fly. Parents bring food to the chicks, but in time the chicks feed themselves.

JUVENILE The teens leave the area of their parents when they are 40 days of age to join a winter flock away from their parents' territory. They are ready the following spring to mate and raise their own young.

Did You Know?

Do Boreal Chickadees remember where they store their winter snacks? Biologists don't think so. Instead, chickadees and their next-door neighbors hide so much winter food that they borrow and share, never noticing which is the owner. In years when there is an outbreak of spruce budworms in the coniferous forest, more Boreal Chickadees are around. Foresters have a message for these worm-eaters: Thank you!

When
Diurnal. They feed during the day and rest at night.

Migration
Permanent resident. During the summer breeding season, they are in pairs, nesting and raising young. The rest of the year they flock together.

Nesting
Nest in the coniferous forests of the north beginning late May–June.

Getting Around
Boreal Chickadees hop from branch to branch and on the ground in search of insects. Short flights between trees are straight and quick. Look for the chickadee's tail to point up when it lands, making a V with its body. It quickly lowers its tail for balance.

Where to Look
Coniferous and boreal forests of north-central and NE Minnesota.
· Beltrami State Forest
· Sax-Zim Bog
· Superior Nat'l Forest
· Nemadji State Forest
· Fond du Lac State Forest
· Zippel Bay State Pk

Year-round Migration	Summer Winter

Purple Finch

Carpodacus purpureus

Length: 5–6 inches
Wingspan: 10 inches

female

Crest can be raised, like a spiked feather-do

Females do not have any red. They are gray with streaks of dark brown, a white eyebrow stripe and white belly. Young look like the female.

Back, head and throat are the color of raspberry fruit-drink

White belly and undertail

Notched tail

"Twitter-twee, twitter-twee!" Warbling song sung by males in late winter to spring. Showing off to females!

Eating Out of the Palm of Your Hand!

You can have Purple Finches and other birds eating out of your hand! Use materials from around the house and make a buddy bird feeder. Stuff old jeans, a long-sleeved shirt and old gloves with recycled papers. Make a head with a gourd or pumpkin using fruit on toothpicks for the eyes, nose and mouth. Get silly, put peanut butter or suet on top of an old hat. Lean your buddy against a tree or bush. Birds feel comfortable near cover. Fill an old baking pan or low basket with thistle, sunflower and millet seeds. Place it on the buddy's lap. In time, birds will get used to the buddy. You can then sit quietly beside it. Next, put the seeds in your lap and the hat on your head. Birds may snack on you!

Habitat Café

Today's Special
willow catkins

Yumm . . . bring an order of beetles, bugs, caterpillars, spiders, grapes, box elder seeds, buds and blossoms of wild cherry and plum trees, and aspen and willow catkins. Purple Finches are omnivorous.

SPRING, SUMMER, FALL MENU:
Mostly seeds, buds and blossoms, some insects

WINTER MENU:
Almost all seeds, a few insects

Life Cycle

NEST The female builds the tidy nest cup 5–60 feet above the ground hidden on a coniferous branch or in the fork of a small tree. She weaves grasses, twigs and bark strips into a shallow bowl and lines it with soft, fine grasses and rabbit, snowshoe hare or deer fur.

EGGS About ¾ inch long. The female incubates the clutch of 3–5 eggs for 12–14 days.

MOM! DAD! Altricial. Both Mom and Dad feed the chicks and remove the fecal sacs from the nest—diaper duty.

NESTLING Chicks are fed regurgitated (partly digested and spit back up) seeds. Finches are one of the few songbirds that feed seeds rather than insects to their young.

FLEDGLING The young have their feathers and can fly short distances when they leave the nest at 13–16 days of age.

JUVENILE Teenagers are mature enough the following spring to date, mate, nest and raise their own young.

Birding Tip

Do birds need the extra seed from backyard bird feeders? Birds can generally survive without the extra food, but it comes in handy when they are fattening up for fall migration, recovering in the spring or feeding chicks. Long, cold winters can make finding food and water tough for birds that stay all year. Once you start providing food and water, keep it up so you can enjoy the birds. Bring these neighbors close enough to get to know them by name!

When
Diurnal. Active during the day and rests at night.

Migration
Permanent resident. During the summer, they nest in northeast Minnesota's coniferous forests. By late October, they begin to travel to central and eastern regions of the state, including backyard bird feeders in the Twin Cities area. This movement peaks again in March–May as they move back to the northern coniferous forests to nest.

Nesting
Purple Finches begin to nest in May in Minnesota.

Getting Around
Purple Finches hop and walk when on the ground. They flit from branch to branch in short flights. In long-distance travel they have an up-and-down, bouncing flight as they flap their wings and then fold them.

Where to Look
Coniferous forests, mixed deciduous-coniferous forests, and open bog areas. They visit coniferous trees in backyards.
· Chippewa Nat'l Forest
· Itasca State Pk
· Superior Nat'l Forest
· Tamarac Nat'l Wildlife Refuge

Year-round	Summer
Migration	Winter

Red-breasted Nuthatch

Sitta canadensis

Length: 5–6 inches
Wingspan: 11 inches

female

Female wears a gray cap and gray eye-stripe. Red color below is pale.

Blue-gray above and red-cinnamon below

Male wears a black cap

Black eyes hidden in a black stripe; white eyebrow stripe.

Juveniles look like pale versions of adults

White chin

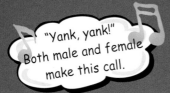

"Yank, yank!" Both male and female make this call.

Fancy Forest Footwork

Head up, head down, turn around…. How does a Red-breasted Nuthatch perform this fancy footwork? It has specially designed feet and toes. The first toe (hallux) is pointed to the back and the other three toes are jointed at the base and pointed forward. Like a mountaineer uses a pick when climbing up or down a steep slope, a nuthatch uses its hallux (first toe). While one foot is being moved, the hallux on the other foot is mounted into tree bark like a pick for support. When you see this tree climber upside down and headfirst, be amazed, he/she is an experienced climber!

Habitat Café

Yumm... bring an order of forest insects and seeds. Red-breasted Nuthatches are insectivores and granivores (seed eaters). Fill your bird feeders with seeds and suet for these backyard visitors.

Today's Special
peanut butter topped with sunflower seeds
BIRD FEEDER TREAT

SPRING, SUMMER, FALL MENU:
Mostly insects, some seeds

WINTER MENU:
More seeds than summer, but still mostly insects

Life Cycle

NEST Both parents hollow out a hole in a soft branch or stub of a dead tree, 5–40 feet above the ground. They may recycle a woodpecker hole. The deep hole is built up with shredded bark, grass and leaves. Mom lines the nest with feathers, fur and moss. A mat of sticky tree sap is put around the hole.

EGGS Almost ¾ inch long. The female incubates the clutch of 4–7 eggs for 12 days.

MOM! DAD! Altricial. With gummy resin around the nest hole, parents do not enter the nest after the first week. Instead, the young open their beaks close to the entrance hole for food delivery. Chicks poke their little rumps out of the nest for fecal sac (diaper) pick-up.

NESTLING Just before the young leave the nest, Mom and Dad put clumps of mammal fur on the sticky resin of the entrance hole.

FLEDGLING They leave the nest at 18–21 days of age.

JUVENILE They stay with Mom and Dad for two more weeks. They are able to fly, feed themselves and search out other teens to form winter flocks during winter months.

Gross Factor

What is that white stuff on your car window? Bird droppings. Three kinds of wastes leave a bird's body in one package. The dark part is the feces (food waste from the intestine). The white part is waste from the blood, filtered out by the kidneys, urates and urine. Birds have the ability to conserve water by making their urine concentrated and chalky rather than liquid. What kind of bird left the dropping? Berry- and seed-eaters may have purple or green droppings. Insect- or animal-eaters often have darker brown parts to their droppings. Gross.

When
Diurnal. They feed during the day and rest at night.

Migration
Permanent resident to short-distance migrant. Move around Minnesota with the changing seasons. In fall, winter and early spring they move to wooded areas with the most food sources. Some may move to central and southern parts of the state or even out of state to the south. They return to the northern forests in spring to nest.

Nesting
Begin nesting in the northern coniferous forests in late May–June.

Getting Around
Zooming through the forests, this bird stops only to pick up a seed or insect. It wedges the seed in a tree bark crack and hacks it open with blows from its sharp bill. Zoooom, it is off again in its fast, short flight to another tree!

Where to Look
Coniferous forest of north-central and NE Minnesota.
· Beltrami Island State Forest
· Superior Nat'l Forest
· Wolf Ridge Env Learning Ctr
· Zippel Bay State Pk

Year-round	Summer
Migration	Winter

White-throated Sparrow

Zonotrichia albicollis

Length: 6–7 inches
Wingspan: 9 inches

tan striped

White line over the eye with a yellow spot between its eye and bill

Black and white or tan with white stripes over top of head

The square white throat patch gives this bird its name

Brown back

Females and males look the same

Gray underside

Juveniles are more dull colored than adults without a throat patch

"Old Sam Pea-body, Pea-body, Pea-body." Translation: "This is my space."

Color-coded Birds

Hold tight, these birds are color-coded by the stripes on top of their head. Why? It appears to determine which birds are more aggressive and defend their territory and which ones are homebodies and take care of the young ones. White stripes identify a strong territory defender. Tan stripes identify a homebody. How does this work? Males almost always pair up with an opposite color female. This ensures that one is home with the kids while the other is keeping out intruders. It doesn't make any difference which is the male or female. Females with white head stripes even sing the male territory song. Tan-striped females do not. Get out your binoculars—color-coded birds may be in the area.

Habitat Café

Yumm . . . bring an order caterpillars, ants, beetles, bugs, spiders, snails and the fruit, berries and seeds of plants. White-throated Sparrows are omnivorous.

Today's Special
snails

SPRING, SUMMER, FALL MENU:
Equal amounts of insects and seeds

WINTER MENU:
Lots of seeds, a few insects

Life Cycle

NEST The female builds the bulky nest cup within three feet of the ground. Often, it is hidden in thick ferns, on a low tree branch, or a small bush. She weaves pine needles, grass, twigs, bark and moss together. The nest is lined with fine, soft grass and fur.

EGGS About ¾ inch long. The female incubates the clutch of 4–5 eggs for 11–14 days.

MOM! DAD! Altricial. Both parents feed the young protein-rich insects. When the chicks turn with their backside to Mom and Dad, the parents take the hint and catch a fresh fecal sac (chick diaper).

NESTLING Parents shade the chicks from the sun and rain by standing over them and spreading their wings.

FLEDGLING The chicks are helpless, unable to walk or hop until they are 7 days of age when they begin to leave the nest. At three weeks of age, they follow their parents, flying among low branches.

JUVENILE On their spring return, they are mature enough to date, mate, nest and raise more White-throated Sparrows!

Birding Tip

Invite wildlife to your backyard. Provide what animals need: food, water, shelter and a place to nest and raise their young. Plant an American Mountain Ash tree and a Viburnum bush. White-throated Sparrows like to eat seeds and fruit. Scatter cracked corn, sunflower seed, peanut chips and safflower seeds on the ground under a bush or low tree. White-throated Sparrows live in the lower levels of the forest edges. Make your yard a welcome place for wildlife.

When

Diurnal. They feed during the day and rest at night.

Migration

Spring Arrival: mid-April
Fall Departure: late Sept.–Oct.
Short-distance migrant. Migrates in small flocks at night to the southern U.S. and northern Mexico. Migrating at night allows for calmer wind, fewer predators and the need for less water since they are out of the sun's heat. In fall and early spring they can be found all over the state.

Nesting

Begins nesting in late May–June in northern Minnesota.

Getting Around

White-throated Sparrows hop on the ground and through forest plants scratching the ground for food. They glean (pick up) insects from plants. They use quick wingbeats as they fly around tree branches.

Where to Look

Coniferous forest of north-central and NE Minnesota. Prefers the undergrowth and forest edges.
· Bear Lake State Pk
· Zippel Bay State Pk
· Tamarac Nat'l Wildlife Refuge
· Superior Nat'l Forest
· Sawbill Trail
    · Itasca State Pk
    · Sax-Zim Bog

Year-round Migration	Summer Winter

Dark-eyed Junco

Junco hyemalis

Length: 6–7 inches
Wingspan: 9–10 inches

female

Females look like males but are duller with brown back and sides

Bill is pale orange-pink

Males are dark gray with a white belly

White outer tail feathers. "Signal of white—a Junco in flight"

"Chack" means "This is my territory." Both males and females give this defense call in all seasons.

Zelda-like Battles

Watch your bird feeders for flocks of 10–20 Dark-eyed Juncos during their fall and spring migration. Pick out the dominant head honcho of the flock. This male sleeks down his head and neck feathers, pushes his neck out and leaps toward other males. The little guys give in or get pecked on the head. Ouch! When two flocks meet, the head honchos may have a battle. The winner is decided in a "head dance." The two males meet face-to-face with legs and heads stretched tall and bills pointed to the sky. Kew. Kew. Clawing and using their bills as swords, they have a standoff, spreading their tails like peacocks. Watching this could be better than a game of Zelda! (O.K., I said could be.)

Habitat Café

Yumm . . . bring an order of grasshoppers, ants, beetles, caterpillars, spiders and weed seeds. Dark-eyed Juncos are omnivorous. Scatter white proso millet on the ground or snow. Watch for juncos!

SPRING MENU:
More insects than seeds

SUMMER, FALL, WINTER MENU:
Mostly seeds, some insects

Today's Special
black oil sunflower seeds
BIRD FEEDER TREAT

Life Cycle

NEST The female builds the nest cup on the ground hidden in thick weeds or up to 8 feet above the ground in a tree or bush. She weaves grass, bark strips, moss and twigs together for the base of the nest cup. It is lined with fine grass, rootlets and mammal fur.

EGGS About ¾ inch long. The female incubates the clutch of 3–5 eggs for 12–13 days. Mom may help the chicks hatch by pulling the eggshell with her bill. She may then eat the shell to help replace the calcium she used to produce the eggs. Eggshells also give her the needed calcium to make a second brood of eggs.

MOM! DAD! Altricial. Both parents hunt for insects, take turns with diaper duty and defend the nest and young against predators.

FLEDGLING Young leave the nest when they are 10–12 days of age. They can feed themselves and fly as well as an adult when they are 25–26 days of age.

JUVENILE Youngsters look like adults but with more brown than gray. At one year of age, they are mature enough to date, mate and raise their own young.

Unsolved Mystery

Bill wiping: While perched on a branch, Juncos wipe each side of their bill from the base to the tip against the branch. Often they wipe their bill before searching for insects. Why? Another unsolved mystery!

When

Dark-eyed Juncos are diurnal. They feed during the day and rest at night.

Migration

Spring Arrival: late March–April Fall Departure: Sept.–Oct. Short-distant migrant. Juncos migrate at night, low to the ground. In the fall, some move to areas in central and southern Minnesota while others fly as far south as the Gulf of Mexico. In general, males winter farther north than females.

Nesting

Dark-eyed Juncos nest in the coniferous forests of NE Minnesota during May–July. They raise 1–2 broods each year.

Getting Around

Juncos hop forward and sideways on the ground scratching and foraging for insects and seeds. They fly with steady, quick wing beats. When flying against the wind, Juncos stay close to the ground. Flying in the same direction of the wind calls for a higher flight that allows the wind to "blow" them along.

Where to Look

Northern coniferous forests during the summer.
· Sawbill Trail
· Gunflint Trail
· Sax-Zim Bog

Year-round Migration	Summer Winter

Evening Grosbeak

Coccothraustes vespertinus

Length: 7–8 inches
Wingspan: 14 inches

Male has black cap and yellow "eyebrow"

female

Females are dull gray with yellow underneath, white rump and white on their black tail. Young look like females with a grayish bill.

Yellow belly and undertail

Black wings and tail

"Clee—ip!"
Loud call heard when a group of grosbeaks visit a bird feeder.

Gross Factor of Another Kind

Gross means disgusting, icky. Gross can also mean big and bulky. This is the perfect way to tell about the big, thick bill of the Evening Grosbeak. Why do they need such a big bill? It works like a pair of large, strong pliers to crack open hard seeds, including cherry pits. Grosbeaks toss the outer cherry fruit that you would eat to the side and eat the soft food inside the hard pit. Each spring, the outer yellow layer of their beak falls off, like a snake sheds its skin. A new green bill is a clue that the Evening Grosbeak you are watching is an adult ready to open hard seeds. Crack!

Habitat Café

Yumm . . . bring an order of pine, fir, red cedar, elderberry and spruce tree seeds with a side order of caterpillars, spiders and beetles. Evening Grosbeaks are omnivorous. Their bird feeder favorites are safflower seeds, black oil sunflower seeds and peanuts.

SPRING, SUMMER, FALL, WINTER MENU:
Mostly seeds, some insects

Today's Special

spruce budworms

Life Cycle

NEST The female builds the loose nest cup 20–60 feet above the ground in spruce and northern white cedar swamps. She weaves together twigs with moss and lichens, lining the inside with rootlets.

EGGS About 1 inch long. The female incubates the clutch of 3–4 eggs for 12–14 days.

MOM! DAD! Altricial. Both parents feed the young by regurgitating (spitting back up) partially digested insect larvae.

NESTLING Starting after the first week, the young eat whole insects and soft seeds on their own.

FLEDGLING Young leave the nest when they are 14 days of age. Mom and Dad stay around and will shell seeds from bird feeders for the kids.

JUVENILE The teens are adult-size and able to fly and feed on their own at 3 months of age.

History Hangout

In April of 1823 near Sault Ste. Marie, Michigan Territory, a young Ojibwe boy heard the strange call of a black and yellow bird that ate the seeds of trees and fruits. The bird was given the Ojibwe name *Pashcundamo* from *pashca-un*, meaning soft, fleshy vegetable. From this the native name Berry-breaker was formed. In 1823, a U.S. agent recording land boundaries heard a bird calling at sunset. Later, in 1825, ornithologist William Cooper named it Finch of the Evening. However, it calls both in the evening and the day.

When

Diurnal. They are active during the day and rest at night.

Migration

Permanent resident. Evening Grosbeaks stay in Minnesota all year, moving from northern parts of the state in the summer, while roaming the state during the fall, winter, and early spring months. Stock your bird feeders; grosbeaks are in large numbers some years and few the next, but nearly always in a group.

Nesting

Evening Grosbeaks nest in Minnesota in June.

Getting Around

Birds that spend a lot of time in trees also hop when on the ground. Look for their side-by-side hopping track pattern as you explore the forest floor. Their flight is undulating (up and down).

Where to Look

Coniferous forests and backyard bird feeders in NE Minnesota.
· Beltrami State Forest
· Itasca State Pk
· Lost River State Forest
· North Woods Audubon Ctr
· Sawbill Trail
· Gunflint Trail

Year-round Migration	Summer Winter

Coniferous Forest Habitat

47

Blue Jay

Cyanocitta cristata

Length: 11–12 inches
Wingspan: 16 inches

raised crest

Blue crest

Black necklace, headband and eyeliner

Blue above and white below

Male and female look alike

White wing bars

Blue tail with black bars and white tips

"Jaay, jaay!" in the Blue Jay's language means "Danger! Join the mob to chase it away!"

The Great Pretender

"Meow." Is this your pet cat, or is it a Blue Jay pretending to be a cat? Great pretenders, Blue Jays can mimic cats, hawks, screech-owls, American Crows, and American Kestrels. This comes in handy. Blue Jays have enemies. They do not like Great Horned Owls hanging around trying to pick them off for lunch. When a Great Horned Owl comes into the area, Blue Jays sound an alarm that mimics a bigger animal, like a hawk. The owl's cover is blown. One jay becomes a very loud and aggressive mob of jays and they chase the intruder out of the area. No more owl on the prowl. Mission accomplished!

Habitat Café

Yumm . . . bring an order of insects, spiders, snails, tree frogs, small fish and the eggs and chicks from nests—along with acorns, seeds and berries. Blue Jays are omnivorous.

SPRING, SUMMER, FALL MENU:
Lots of plants, some animal matter

WINTER MENU:
More animal matter than in spring, summer and fall, but still mostly plants

Life Cycle

NEST Both the male and female gather nest materials. The female builds the bulky nest cup 10–20 feet above the ground, hidden most often in a coniferous tree. She weaves bark, twigs, leaves and materials such as string, fabric and paper. The nest is lined with soft rootlets. The male brings her food while she works.

EGGS About 1 inch long. The female incubates the clutch of 4–5 eggs for 16–18 days.

MOM! DAD! Altricial. Dad does most of the feeding. Both parents hunt for food and remove fecal sacs (chick diapers).

NESTLING With eyes closed and naked when they hatch, the chicks have a lot of growing to do. By the seventh day, their eyes are open and feathers are beginning to grow. That is fast growth.

FLEDGLING The young leave the nest when they are 19–21 days old and are able to run along the ground with fluttering hops.

JUVENILE Young Blue Jays resemble their parents but are a bit duller, grayer and browner in color. They are mature enough at one year of age to date, mate, nest and raise their own young.

Gross Factor

Do birds have flatulence (pass gas)? Blue Jays do. Adult Blue Jays were observed passing gas by a biologist who was studying them (Weisbrod 1965). Now you know even more about bird bodily functions. Word has it that they have a "hiccup" call, too. Silly birds.

When

Diurnal. Blue Jays are active during the day and rest at night.

Migration

Permanent resident. Blue Jays stay in Minnesota all year. Some leave the colder northern forests to spend winter in the central or southern parts of the state. Watch for groups of jays in the fall to spring as they move around looking for a tasty meal. To prepare for winter, they store acorns in the fall. A Blue Jay may store several thousand nuts or acorns each fall! This helps new oak trees to sprout, making Blue Jays an important part of the forest cycle.

Nesting

Blue Jays begin to nest in mid-April–May in Minnesota.

Getting Around

Watch below the treetops for a Blue Jay to glide on its short, rounded wings with white-tipped tail fanned out; it's getting ready to land. During longer flights to gather acorns, as well as migration, Blue Jays fly above the treetops.

Where to Look

Mature, older deciduous, mixed deciduous-coniferous forests often near a river or lake.
· A *Super Adaptor*

Year-round	Summer
Migration	Winter

Gray Jay

Perisoreus canadensis

Length: 11–13 inches
Wingspan: 18 inches

Short, black bill is used to twist and tug meat from a dead animal

No crest on head

Gray feathers camouflage the jay against the gray bark of a coniferous tree

Pale gray chest

Male and female look alike; juveniles are dark gray

"Koke-ke-keer!" This scolding call can be heard more than a quarter of a mile away.

Hiding the Loot

Have you ever saved your ABC (Already Been Chewed) gum in a favorite spot for later? Then you and the Gray Jay have something in common. Gray Jays have a special throat pouch to carry food in and an extra large salivary (spit) gland. They stick their favorite food together with thick and sticky saliva and then glue it to a tree. If they think another jay has discovered their hiding spot, they will move the food to a different place and jam a piece of bark or lichen over it. When the snow blows and the hungries hit, a frozen dinner is ready, allowing this robber bird to survive well in the harsh, cold winters of the north.

Habitat Café

Today's Special
suet, seeds
and fruit
BIRD FEEDER TREAT

Yumm . . . bring an order of butterflies, grasshoppers, beetles, bugs, spiders, ticks, mice, voles, the eggs and young of small birds, blueberries, mushrooms, soft seeds and dead animal meat. Gray Jays are omnivorous. They eat almost any small living thing in the northern forest.

SPRING, SUMMER, FALL, WINTER MENU:
Any available food item

Life Cycle

NEST The female builds the bulky (8-inch diameter) nest cup hidden in the branches of a coniferous tree. It is usually 6–12 feet above the ground.

EGGS About 1⅛ inches long. The female incubates the clutch of 2–5 eggs for 16–18 days.

MOM! DAD! Altricial. Both parents feed the chicks and take turns removing the fecal sacs—chick diaper duty.

NESTLING Mom and Dad bring spit-covered "baby food" wads in their cheek pouches. Each glob of food is pushed out of their throat and into the chick's gaping beak. The dark brown wads contain insects high in protein. Double yum!

FLEDGLING The young leave the nest when they are 23 days of age.

JUVENILE Teens stay in the area with their parents until June, when they are 55–65 days of age. The strongest bird then chases its brothers and sisters out of the area. When spring comes, Mom and Dad chase away this offspring. It's time for their last "chick" to find its own space in the forest to date, mate, nest and raise more jays.

Did You Know?

When you spy a moose, take a close look for a Gray Jay giving it a free cleaning. Jays eat ticks from the moose's hide. There's a black fly… gulp. They catch annoying black flies from an antler perch also. Tasty little morsels.

When
Gray Jays are diurnal. They feed by day and rest at night.

Migration
Permanent resident. Some Gray Jays move along the North Shore of Lake Superior in October.

Nesting
Gray Jays nest in the coniferous forests of NE Minnesota during March–April. An early nesting season gives young Gray Jays time to mature and learn the skills of food catching before the cold winter begins.

Getting Around
Gray Jays are skilled at sneaking up! They perch near prey and scout out the scene (including the baked beans on your picnic plate). Before you know they're even around, they glide on quiet wings, pick up the loot with their bill, and transfer it to their feet for a quick getaway. Sneaky antics have earned Gray Jays the nickname "Camp Robber."

Where to Look
Coniferous forest of north-central and NE Minnesota.
· Beltrami State Forest
· Moose-Willow Wildlife Mgmt Area
· Fond du Lac State Forest
· Lost River State Forest
· Nemadji State Forest
· Superior Nat'l Forest
· Zippel Bay State Pk

Year-round Migration	Summer Winter

Spruce Grouse

Falcipennis canadensis

Length: 13–16 inches
Wingspan: 22 inches

Male has bright red, bare skin above each eye

female

Females are smaller than males. They do not have red-skinned eyebrows. They are more rust with closely spaced black and rust bars around the body.

Beak is used to grip food and rip it from the plant with a jerk of the head

Males are brown, gray, and black patterned with a black throat ruff

Barred and white-spotted black tail with a rusty band at end

"Drum, drum...." Males saying, *"This is my space."*

Dancing to Their Own Drum

Explore Superior National Forest in the spring and hear a drum coming from—where? Male Spruce Grouse are ventriloquists. Their drumbeats echo over the forest, making it hard to decide where they are performing their mating drum and dance routine. Make your way to an open area in a spruce bog. With head drawn back, red "eyebrows" puffed out, tail spread and wings lowered and open, males boogie! Strutting on short legs, they suddenly fly up a few feet. Their wings beat just fast enough to hold them in the same place for a moment, sending low drumbeats over the damp forest. They float back down to the ground, pleased to have danced to the beat of their own drum.

Habitat Café

Yumm . . . bring an order of coniferous tree buds and tender pine and spruce needles, cranberry buds and fruit, blueberries and juniper berries. Spruce Grouse are herbivores. Bacteria and protozoa in their digestive system change the cellulose in tree needles to sugar!

SPRING, SUMMER, FALL, WINTER MENU:
Lots of tree buds, needles and berries

Today's Special
mushrooms

Life Cycle

NEST The female makes a shallow, camouflaged nest on the ground, hidden near a low-hanging spruce branch or in a bush. She may line the nest with grass, leaves, spruce needles and feathers.

EGGS About 1¾ inches long. The female incubates the clutch of 6–8 eggs for 17–24 days. She takes recesses to find food.

MOM! DAD! Precocial. Newly hatched chicks walk around as soon as they are dry to look for a meal of insects. Mom stays near the chicks and broods them at night.

The young stray farther and farther from Mom, eventually leaving the family brood to find their own space in September. They may loaf in the sun and take a dust bath to get rid of pesky insects.

JUVENILE At one year of age, they are mature enough to date, mate, nest and raise their own young.

Unsolved Mystery

In 1870, T. Martin Truppe worked as a surveyor for the Northern Pacific Railroad. His wildlife notes included Spruce Grouse as abundant and breeding in the central part of the state from Carlton County west to the Mississippi River. During this time, Spruce Grouse were numerous as far south as Mille Lacs Lake and west as far as the coniferous forest extended. In 1932, Thomas Roberts noted that Spruce Grouse were only found from the Lake of the Woods on the border of Canada to Lake Superior. What caused this decline? Solve this history mystery!

When

Diurnal. Food eaten late in the day is stored in the grouse's crop. During the night when the birds do not eat, the food stored in the crop is digested and used as heat energy.

Migration

Permanent resident. Spruce Grouse have seasonal movements from nesting to wintering areas according to where there is the most food.

Nesting

Spruce Grouse nest in the coniferous forests of northern Minnesota during June.

Getting Around

Spruce Grouse fly fast and silent in short distances from tree to tree to forage and escape predators. Like Ruffed Grouse, they grow extra scales on the sides of their feet in the fall that act like snowshoes on snow. The scales may also help the bird walk along tree branches when feeding. They can fly above the browse line of moose, deer and snowshoe hares to find food other animals cannot reach.

Where to Look

North of Lake Superior in jack pine, white spruce, balsam fir, tamarack and white cedar swamps and bogs.

| Year-round | Summer |
| Migration | Winter |

Ruffed Grouse

Bonasa umbellus

Length: 15–19 inches
Wingspan: 22 inches

Ruff and comb feathers are fanned out when drumming or threatened

drumming

female

Males are brown, gray or rust above with streaks of white

Females look like males but tail bands are not as clear. Tail, crest and ruff are shorter.

Male has two or more white dots on rump feathers; female has one dot. Male's banded brown tail is fanned when drumming.

There are up to 50 wing beats in one 10-second drum...drum...drum roll.

Let It Snow...

How do grouse stay warm in Minnesota's frigid winters? They pull up a blanket and snuggle in—a blanket of snow. Snow is one of nature's best insulators with tiny pockets of air that trap the heat of the grouse like a blanket. Watch out for snow-plowing grouse as they fly into soft snow from a tree, making an invisible burrow that is both warm and safe from predators. Getting around on top of snow requires a change in footwear. Each fall, grouse grow scale-like fringes on the sides of their feet that work like snowshoes. The extra width of the scales spreads their weight over a larger surface area allowing the bird to walk on top of the snow. Put on your snowshoes—explore!

Habitat Café

Yumm . . . bring an order of aspen and poplar buds and twigs, leaves and seeds with a side of berries and other fruits during the summer. Ruffed Grouse are herbivores, but they feed only insects to their chicks.

SPRING, SUMMER, FALL MENU:
Mostly seeds, some tree buds and twigs

WINTER MENU:
Lots of tree buds and twigs, a few seeds

Today's Special
aspen and poplar tree buds and twigs

Life Cycle

NEST The female builds a simple nest on the ground at the base of a tree or under the slant a large rock, log or tree root. The nest is lined with leaves, pine needles and a few grouse feathers.

EGGS About 1½ inches long. The female incubates the clutch of 9–12 eggs for 21–24 days.

MOM! DAD! Precocial. The chicks are out of their egg and on the run right away. Mom leads them to areas with insects for the first 12 weeks. She broods the chicks at night and during cold, wet weather until their bodies are able to make enough heat energy of their own (3 weeks of age).

By the time they are 10–12 days old, the chicks add flying to their activities. During the first two weeks, most of the chicks' diet is insects that they catch on their own. By the time they are two months old, they eat mostly tree buds, fruit and seeds.

JUVENILE In late August and early September, when they are 12 weeks of age, they leave the family group and go their own way. Teens look like Mom, without the dark tail bands.

Do the Math

When the air is -27 degrees above the snow surface, it will be +24 degrees seven inches below the surface of the snow. How many degrees difference does the layer of snow cause? Do the math: ____ degrees difference. This is why a winter with little snow is actually unfavorable to grouse survival.

Bring on the snow! Answer on pages 194-195.

When
Diurnal. They feed during the day and rest at night.

Migration
Permanent resident. Ruffed Grouse stay in Minnesota year-round.

Nesting
Ruffed Grouse start drumming as early as March and begin nesting in May in northern and southeastern parts of Minnesota.

Getting Around
Ruffed Grouse walk on the ground and on the branches of trees and shrubs when foraging and feeding. Their flight is short with a quick burst of speed, followed by a glide to the ground, tree or shrub. Their short and rounded wings are made for fast takeoffs and turns around trees.

Where to Look
Coniferous and deciduous forests with aspen trees.
· Dorer Forest
· Tamarac Nat'l Wildlife Refuge
· Nerstrand State Pk
· Chippewa Nat'l Forest
· Superior Nat'l Forest Natural Hist. Area
· Moose-Willow Wildlife Mgmt Area
· Roseau Bog Wildlife Mgmt Area
· Whitewater Wildlife Mgmt Area

Year-round Migration	Summer Winter

Coniferous Forest Habitat

55

Great Gray Owl

Strix nebulosa

Length: 22–23 inches
Wingspan: 4–5 feet

listening for prey

in flight

Yellow eyes and bill

Black chin with white bow tie

Females are generally larger than males

Male and female look alike

Take away the dense feather mass and this owl is taller but lighter than its northern cousin, the Snowy Owl

Long 8–12-inch tail allows owls to move around trees to catch prey

"Who-oo-oo-oo?" Listen for this deep call during the mating season, when male and female owls pair up.

I Hear You!

Finding food is a big deal to owls. To a Great Gray Owl, food means catching Meadow Voles. Look to the face of a Great Gray Owl for a clue to how they find small mammals. Their facial feathers are arranged like a satellite disk. This circular pattern funnels sound directly to their ears, located under the feathers on the outside edges of the disk. Your ears are the same height on each side of your head. The owl's ears are each at a different level. To know exactly where a Meadow Vole is in the grass or snow the owl triangulates the sound. Never mind if the snow is deep and crusted. Great Gray Owls dive (called snow plunging) for small mammals under the snow with their head and sharp talons.

Habitat Café

Yumm . . . bring an order of Meadow Voles with a side order of mice, shrews, rabbits and snowshoe hares. This bird is a flying vole-trap. Great Gray Owls are carnivorous.

SPRING, SUMMER, FALL, WINTER MENU:
Mainly voles, a few other mammals

Today's Special
juicy Meadow Voles

Life Cycle

NEST Only up to 50 pairs of Great Gray Owls nest in Minnesota. They do not build their own nest but recycle a hawk, eagle, raven or crow nest in the top of a tall tree. Though they are poor carpenters, the owls may repair an old nest with sticks and a lining of feathers, dry grass and moss.

EGGS About 2 inches long. The female incubates the clutch of 1–9 eggs for 28–36 days.

MOM! DAD! Altricial. Both parents care for the young.

NESTLING The white chicks stay in the nest for up to 21 days.

FLEDGLING Once out of the nest, both parents continue to care for the young until they fledge at about 55 days of age. Mom continues to feed them until they are 4–5 months of age.

JUVENILE Many teens migrate north to Canada. Both immature and adult Great Gray Owls roam except during the nesting-breeding season.

Do the Math

Once every 3–4 years the number of Meadow Voles drops very low in Canada, sending Great Gray Owls south in search of food. Minnesota has had an invasion (high numbers) of Great Gray Owls in the years 2005, 2001, 1997, 1993 and 1989. The following years had an "echo effect" where the number of owls was sometimes about half as high as the invasion year.

Plot the data on a chart or graph and practice your scientific skills. Can you predict the next invasion? Answer on pages 194-195.

When

Crepuscular. Dines most often at sunrise and sunset. Its bright yellow eyes filter light, a possible adaptation to the long summer daylight hours of the Canadian and Arctic regions.

Migration

Boreal migrant. During hard, cold, snowy winters in Canada they move south to Minnesota's boreal forests to find food, sometimes staying to nest.

Nesting

A few Great Gray Owls nest in the coniferous forests of northeast Minnesota in late March–April.

Getting Around

Native Americans living in Alaska gave the Great Gray Owl the name "awkward walker" for its clumsy movements.

Where to Look

Coniferous forest of north-central and NE Minnesota. Dense grassy areas of roadsides, fields and open coniferous forest edges near a water source like a river, bog or stream. Low tree branches, sign posts and poles along roadsides are popular lookouts.
· Superior Nat'l Forest
· Chippewa Nat'l Forest
· Sax-Zim Bog
· Roseau area

Year-round	Summer
Migration	Winter

Snowy Owl

Bubo scandiacus

Length: 21–26 inches
Wingspan: 4–5 feet

Large, yellow eyes

Blue-black, hooked bill

Males are pure white with a few dark spots on their body and wings

Long, broad wings

Feathered, "insulated boots" keep the legs and feet warm. Shiny black talons.

prepare for lift-off

female

Females have heavy brown-gray bars across their wings and body

Immature owls are more heavily marked than females

The Ghosts of Winter

Winter ghosts come to Minnesota on snow-white wings. They come from the arctic tundra (open, flat arctic plains) of Canada in search of food. In years with a bumper crop of lemmings to eat in Canada, Snowy Owls raise a large clutch of young owls and do not migrate south. In years when food is scarce, they raise fewer young and move south for the winter. Minnesota does not have tundra, but watch in an open area for this owl, which can be mistaken for a large chunk of snow—look closer for the yellow eyes. A few migrate to the grain elevator area in the Duluth harbor most years for a regular menu of rodents. Mind your wildlife watching manners and ask before entering private property.

Habitat Café

Yumm . . . bring an order of lemmings, rabbits, snowshoe hares, fish and carrion (dead animal meat). Snowy Owls are 100% carnivorous. Depending on their food supply, owls' lives can be feast or famine. When hunting is good, they can eat 1,600 lemmings in a single year; when times are tough, they can survive up to 40 days without food.

SPRING, SUMMER, FALL, WINTER MENU:
Lemmings, voles, rabbits, fish, carrion

Today's Special
voles

Life Cycle

NEST The female scrapes out a nest in the frozen turf and moss in an open, windswept site. If the nesting area becomes drifted with snow, she may abandon the nest and eggs.

EGGS About 2¼ inches long. The female incubates the clutch of 3–7 eggs for 30–33 days. In years when prey is plentiful she may lay up to 11 eggs.

MOM! DAD! Semi-altricial. The chicks have a gray down that absorbs the heat of the sun and camouflages them from predators. They open their eyes on the fifth day. Dad brings dinner and Mom picks out the soft heart and liver to feed the chicks.

NESTLING The young are able to walk from the nest at 14 days of age but do not leave the nest until they are 25–26 days of age.

FLEDGLING Once out of the nest, Dad brings whole prey to the young. By the time the owlets are on their own, they have eaten over 1,500 lemmings! They can fly well at 50 days of age.

JUVENILE It takes 2–5 years for the young to be mature enough to mate, date, nest and raise their own young.

History Hangout

Snowy Owls have been around long enough to be included in the cave art of the ancient Paleolithic people of Europe. Etched into the rock face of a cave in Les Trois Freres, Ariege, France, is a pair of Snowy Owls and their chicks. The Arctic climate was much farther south than it is today, making France a subarctic habitat for Snowy Owls.

When

Diurnal. They feed during the day and rest at night.

Migration

Boreal migrant. In years when they move into the northern part of the state, they are found from October until March. The peak is in November and December.

Nesting

Snowy Owls do not nest in Minnesota, but move here from Canada for the winter, when food is in short supply.

Getting Around

Be very quiet. Snowy Owls can hear you long before you see them! They perch in a spot where they can see all around. Looking like a patch of snow, they wait patiently for hours without moving, listening for voles and lemmings under the snow. They swoop down over their prey to kill it instantly with needle-sharp talons. Gulp—they eat small prey headfirst and whole. To kill larger prey they peck it on the head.

Where to Look

Search open areas, on river ice and near Lake Superior's shores.
· Roseau Bog
· Superior Nat'l Forest
· Lost River State Forest
· Chippewa Nat'l Forest
· Cedar Creek Natural History Area

Year-round	Summer
Migration	Winter

Deciduous Forest

Birds that live in and around deciduous forests have fascinating adaptations to one of the most diverse habitats in Minnesota. Flight through trees that can outmaneuver a stunt plane...wood drilling to challenge the best of carpenters...songsters that can out-compose Beethoven...disguises that can fool the most clever detectives...and some of the most brilliant blues and reds found in nature.

61

On Again, Off Again

Deciduous trees lose all of their leaves every year and grow new ones. In Minnesota, the species (kinds) of deciduous trees found in a forest depends on the land terrain (hilly, flat, etc.), soil type and climate.

Deciduous forests bordering the lowlands of the Minnesota and Mississippi Rivers contain such giants as cottonwoods and in more mature stands, American elm, black and green ash, silver maple and swamp white oak.

Maple Basswood Forest

The forests along western Minnesota's prairies and open grasslands host transitional shrubs and plants that provide tasty fruits and berries. There are also large, sturdy oaks that brace against the prairie winds with their broad out-stretched limbs, dense wood and deep roots.

Deciduous forests that border and often mix with the coniferous forests of northern Minnesota contain a mixture of hardwoods such as aspen and paper birch; trees that can grow in soils with few nutrients.

Because glaciers left a patchwork of soil types in this area, you'll often see a wide variety of trees and other plants living close together. This creates a diverse habitat for birds and other wildlife, so you never know for sure what type of bird or animal you'll see next!

The large tracts of basswoods and maples of the "Big Woods" written about in early stories of Minnesota still exist but are much smaller than before. The large forests have been broken up, and in many cases replaced by building projects and farm fields.

Colorful Variety

More bird species live in a deciduous forest than on a prairie because there are more habitat levels in a forest. Getting to know the many birds that live in deciduous forests is made easier by exploring the different levels of the forest.

Mixed Boreal Forest

The highest level, the top or upper canopy of trees, includes nests of sky dwellers like owls and hawks. Great Blue Herons (page 182) and Great Egrets (page 180), are water birds with long legs and feet adapted to both wading in shallow water and balancing on tree branches. They take to the tops of deciduous trees in large colonies for building their gangly nests.

Birds that hunt for insects on tree leaves, branches and trunks use the middle level of the forest. So do birds that favor the seeds, fruit and nuts found there. Some birds nest in tree cavities. Others, like tiny carpenters, build nests in branches—some close to the trunk, others at the very tips.

Being able to fly away from predators allows males to wear bright colors during the breeding season when they are trying to "wow" the females right off their perches!

Barred Owl

Protective Camo, Amazing Antics

The ground level of the deciduous forest is home to birds that eat the seeds, nuts and fruit of woodland plants. Some birds prefer the snails, insects and worms found under leaves and in decaying wood.

Male Wild Turkey Strutting

Many of these birds are well camouflaged against the brown and light patterns of the forest floor. Their nests are built in grasses and leaves, under logs, and even in structures that look more like a domed oven than a nest. Males resort to some bizarre and outlandish (more like right off the land!) courtship stunts to capture the flutter of females in this group.

Turn the pages to learn about the birds that make their home in the different levels of Minnesota's deciduous forests. Take this book along and take a walk in the woods with a buddy. For a long walk, you'll need an adult. Remember to tell a grownup where you are going, who is with you and when you will be back. If your plans change, be certain to tell them right away. Safety first!

Check Off the Deciduous Birds You See!

When you spot deciduous birds, use these pages to check them off. The locations of these illustrations indicate where you might see them.

- ☐ House Wren (pg. 66)
- ☐ Indigo Bunting (pg. 68)
- ☐ Black-capped Chickadee (pg. 70)
- ☐ Ovenbird (pg. 72)
- ☐ White-breasted Nuthatch (pg. 74)
- ☐ Downy Woodpecker (pg. 76)
- ☐ Scarlet Tanager (pg. 78)
- ☐ Eastern Bluebird (pg. 80)
- ☐ Baltimore Oriole (pg. 82)
- ☐ Northern Cardinal (pg. 84)
- ☐ Purple Martin (pg. 86)
- ☐ American Robin (pg. 88)
- ☐ American Woodcock (pg. 90)
- ☐ Brown Thrasher (pg. 92)
- ☐ Mourning Dove (pg. 94)
- ☐ Cooper's Hawk (pg. 96)
- ☐ Pileated Woodpecker (pg. 98)
- ☐ Barred Owl (pg. 100)
- ☐ Great Horned Owl (pg. 102)
- ☐ Wild Turkey (pg. 104)

House Wren

Troglodytes aedon

Length: 4–5 inches
Wingspan: 6 inches

Fairly long, slender, down-curved bill for picking up insects

The young look like their parents

Short wings that are curved in on the underside

Males and females are brown above and light brown below

Narrow tail that is held up, down or fanned out depending on the signal

"Tsi, tsi, tsi, oodle-oodle-oodle-oodle." When the male's warbling song becomes shorter and quieter, it is a sure sign that the chicks have hatched.

Carpenter of the Forest

The pocket of a scarecrow's overalls, an overturned clay flowerpot, a boot left outside, a mailbox, an abandoned woodpecker hole, a deep crack in a rotten tree—all are used by House Wrens for a house. Watch wrens long enough and you can add to this remarkable list. Building and putting up backyard wren houses is the best invitation you can give to these small birds. Males prepare 2–7 houses for a female to choose from. Before she arrives, he is busy spring cleaning, bringing in furniture (small twigs) and setting out snacks (spider egg cases and larvae). How will you know which house is "Home Sweet Home?" When the female adds grass and feather pillows to her favorite cozy house.

Habitat Café

Today's Special
mealworms

Yumm . . . bring an order of leafhoppers, grasshoppers, crickets, caterpillars, beetles, moths, ants, bugs and spiders. House Wrens are insectivores. The parents will eat snail shells for the grit and feed snail shells to their chicks for the calcium content.

SPRING, SUMMER, FALL, WINTER MENU:
Almost entirely insects

Life Cycle

NEST The female finishes the nest started by the male making an average of 300 trips to the nest in only a few days. She lines the nest with grass, fur, hair and feathers.

EGGS About ½ inch long. The female lays one egg each day for 6–8 days. Full-time incubation starts after the last egg is laid and continues for 12–15 days. Mom does all the incubation. All the eggs hatch on the same day.

MOM! DAD! Altricial. At first, Dad "beaks" the insects over to Mom and she feeds the chicks. After the first days, they both feed the chicks, remove fecal sacs (diaper duty) and carry the sacs away from the nest.

NESTLING The downy chicks stay in the nest for 12–18 days.

FLEDGLING Young wrens leave the nest at 17–18 days of age. For another two weeks, the parents bring the kids insects.

JUVENILE In late August they prepare to migrate. On their spring return, they are mature enough to breed and raise their own young.

Did You Know?

How do bird eggs stay warm? Incubating parents have a brood patch. This bare spot on the bird's belly has many blood vessels close to the skin's surface. During incubation, the blood flow to this area increases, making it a real "hot spot." The parent sits with the eggs directly under the brood patch. Once the parent's job of keeping eggs and chicks warm is finished, feathers regrow and the brood patch disappears.

When

House Wrens are diurnal. They feed during the day and rest at night.

Migration

Spring Arrival: mid April–May
Fall Departure: mid Aug.–Sept.
The House Wren is a short-distance migrant to the southern U.S. and Mexico.

Nesting

In Minnesota, begin nesting in May. Raise 1–2 broods per year. Nest territories are ½–¾ of an acre in size.

Getting Around

House Wrens hop on the ground and fly low from bush to bush in search of insects. Their longer flights are straight and steady. Tail signals: A wren's tail in the straight-up position is a signal the bird feels excited or in danger. Tail down means it is comfortable. A male with a fanned out and lowered tail, head held forward, and fluffed up back feathers, is defending his territory.

Where to Look

Open shrubby woodlands, edges including backyards and parks all over Minnesota.
· A *Super Adaptor*

Year-round	Summer
Migration	Winter

Deciduous Forest Habitat

Indigo Bunting

Passerina cyanea

Length: 5–5½ inches
Wingspan: 8 inches

Black eyes

male

female

Females are pale brown with light wing bars

The male is deep blue in the breeding season; during the rest of the year, he is brown with a tan underside and a blue rump.

"Indigo" means "blue" but these buntings are actually brown. The blue color is light reflecting off the top layer of the feathers. The true brown-gray feather color can be seen when sunlight is not directly on the feathers.

Black legs

"Fire-fire, where-where, here-here, see-it, see-it." The male's spring and summer song. First-year males learn from a male next door.

Night Migration

How do Indigo Buntings know which direction to fly during night migration? Do they use the stars as a map? To find an answer, scientists placed young birds in a planetarium (star theater) and exposed them to the rotation of stars that occur in winter, spring, summer and fall. The birds turned to the north in the "spring" and to the south in the "fall." Were the stars the only clue to finding north and south? Birds also turned north and south based on their hormones (body chemicals). Shifts in hormone levels were triggered by changes in the amount of daylight. Hormone levels may be why some bird species start gaining and storing extra fat and get "restless" a few weeks before migration.

Habitat Café

Yumm . . . bring an order of grasshoppers, caterpillars, beetles, seeds and berries. Indigo Buntings are omnivorous. They glean (pick up) insects from plants.

SPRING, SUMMER, FALL MENU:
Mainly insects, some seeds and berries

WINTER MENU:
Lots of seeds and buds, a few insects

Life Cycle

NEST The female builds a nest cup in the branches of a shrub just 1–3 feet above the ground. She weaves strips of bark, grass stems and leaves together. Spider webs are woven in and out to hold the grasses and leaves together. The inside is lined with fine grasses, rootlets and animal hair/fur.

EGGS About ½ inch long. The female incubates the clutch of 3–4 eggs for 11–12 days.

MOM! DAD! Altricial. Mom does the chick care in this family. Dad is nearby calling out warnings to predators to stay far away.

NESTLING While Mom is out of the nest getting food, the young huddle together to stay warm and save energy.

FLEDGLING Young buntings leave the nest at nine days of age.

JUVENILE Juvenile buntings flock together and prepare for fall migration. During the first year, young males may be brown or a brown-blue mix with white wing bar.

Unsolved Mystery

Science is about solving mysteries. Using the same scientific method you use to do a science fair project, scientists pose a question and hypothesis, design experiments to test it and study the results (data). Did the results answer the question or provide clues? What is the conclusion? Scientists use the new information to make our world a better place to live. Detective work is waiting for you. Enter your school science fair and solve a mystery!

When

Indigo Buntings are diurnal. They feed during the day and rest at night.

Migration

Spring Arrival: May
Fall Departure: September
Long-distance migrant by night over the Gulf of Mexico to Central America and Neotropics.

Nesting

Indigo Buntings nest in southern Minnesota during May–June. Record your nest records in Journal Pages.

Getting Around

Indigo Buntings hop from branch to branch and on the ground when searching for insects. Check the bottom of your shoes. Do they have treads that give you better grip when running ? Birds need grip too. Scales on the bottom of their feet allow them to grip tree branches, slippery rocks along lakeshores, and more.

Where to Look

Bushy areas and woodland borders.
· Afton State Pk
· Minnesota River Birding Trail
· Sibley State Pk

Year-round	Summer
Migration	Winter

Deciduous Forest Habitat

Black-capped Chickadee

Poecile atricapillus

Length: 5–6 inches
Wingspan: 8 inches

Short, small, black bill shaped like a cone

Black cap and chin

Weighs only as much as one quarter!

White breast and belly

Gray back

Females and males look the same

Long tail

"Chickadee-dee, Chickadee-dee-dee" means "Hey, I'm over here!" "Fee-bee, fee-bee" is often a male saying, "This is my space!"

Tiny Bird–Mighty Adaptations

Minnesota's deciduous woods are home to a tiny, yet mighty, survivor. The Black-capped Chickadee stays in Minnesota all year. They have adapted to the cold, snowy winters by lowering their body temperature at night. A lower night temperature uses less energy so they can skip the extra trip for a midnight snack. During the day, chickadees fill up on high energy foods and stash snacks for later use. A Minnesota deer hunter watched a group of chickadees each carry away about one pound of deer fat in a single day! They stuffed and pounded it with their small pointed bills into every tree bark hole and crack they could find. A mighty job for a tiny bird.

Habitat Café

Today's Special

spiders

Yumm . . . bring an order of caterpillars and the eggs of gypsy and codling moths. A friend of Minnesota's forests, they eat moths that are destructive to some trees. Black-capped Chickadees are insectivores.

SPRING, SUMMER, FALL MENU:
🐜 Mostly insects, some seeds and berries

WINTER MENU:
🐜 Insects and an equal amount of seeds, berries and fat

Life Cycle

NEST Hole is made in the soft, rotten wood of a tree, 4–10 feet above ground. The female makes the nest lining with rabbit fur, moss, feathers and even the soft threads of insect cocoons. Whether it's the Chickadee's own tree cavity, one made by woodpeckers or a people-made birdhouse, a different nest is used each year.

 EGGS About ½ inch long. The female incubates 6–8 eggs for 12–13 days. The male brings food.

MOM! DAD! Altricial. Both Mom and Dad feed the young and remove the fecal pellets that are contained in a slippery coating. This makes the job of taking them out of the nest easier. Chick diaper duty!

NESTLING The brown-gray down is pushed out, but stays attached to the juvenile feathers until it is worn away after the bird leaves the nest at 16 days of age.

FLEDGLING Their pink feet and bill soon turn black. They look just like an adult at 10 days out of the nest. For the first 3–4 weeks out of the nest, they stay with Mom and Dad.

JUVENILE Juveniles join a small winter flock. At one year of age, they are mature enough to date, mate, nest and raise their own young

Unsolved Mystery

Why are the eggs of many cavity nesting birds white? It's dark inside a cozy tree hole. Some scientists think white eggs are easier for parent birds to see in a nest. Black-capped Chickadee eggs are white with tiny red-brown spots at the larger end. When the parent leaves the nest, the eggs are covered to keep them warm and invisible from predators. The mystery of the white eggs remains unsolved. What ideas do you have?

When
Diurnal. Chickadees feed during the day and rest at night.

Migration
Permanent resident. In winter, chickadees form groups of 6–10 birds, breaking up into pairs in spring. They may also share roost boxes or other large cavities, mixing in groups of up to 50 small birds. On cold winter nights, they squeeze into their own small tree hollows.

Nesting
Chickadees begin excavating nest holes in mid-April, with egg laying and incubation during May–June in Minnesota.

Getting Around
Look for a flash of lighter color on the tips of their gray wings in flight. When they need to escape a predator they can change directions in just .03 of a second! How do they stay hanging upside down while picking insects off the underside of a tree branch? They have special leg muscles. They creep up and down tree trunks and hop from twig to twig.

Where to Look
Deciduous and mixed forests with open edges.
· Backyard birdhouses and feeders

Year-round Migration	Summer Winter

Deciduous Forest Habitat

Ovenbird

Seiurus aurocapilla

Length: 6 inches
Wingspan: 9–10 inches

orange cap

Rusty orange cap with a black rim

Brown on top

White eye-ring

White below with dark brown streaks

Male and female look alike

Pink legs and feet

"Teacher, teacher, teacher, teacher, teacher, teacher" is Ovenbird for "This is my space!"

Head Over Wing in Love

Ovenbirds have a mating song and dance worth trekking to Minnesota's deep forest to watch in June and July. By the light of the sun or moon, the flirting male darts to the top of a tree. From there he dashes through the air in a series of hot-rod zigzags. Shifting speeds, he spreads his wings and coasts gracefully to the forest floor while serenading his gal. Ovenbirds have been doing this head over wing dance for 10,000 years, at least. Will they be able to continue? Since the mid-1900s there are fewer and fewer ovenbirds. Building roads, houses, offices and bigger farms breaks large forests into smaller pieces, called forest fragmentation. Ovenbirds need the deep inside of a forest to survive.

Habitat Café

Yumm . . . bring an order of grasshoppers, ants, beetles, bugs and small seeds. Mom eats the eggshells immediately after the chicks hatch! The shells are like a calcium vitamin to replace the calcium her body used to make the clutch of eggs. Ovenbirds are omnivorous. They eat both plant and animal matter.

SPRING, SUMMER, FALL, WINTER MENU:
Almost entirely insects, some seeds

Today's Special
earthworms

Life Cycle

NEST The female builds the domed nest beginning with a small hollow in the forest floor. Using dead leaves, grass, weed stems, rootlets and moss, she weaves a dome, or upside-down bowl, over the top. She includes a side entrance. On the very inside she makes a cup nest with fine rootlets and animal hair/fur.

EGGS About ⅞ inch long. The female incubates the clutch of 4–5 eggs for 11–14 days.

MOM! DAD! Altricial. Both parents feed insects to the young and do diaper duty by eating the fecal sacs of the young. When young Ovenbirds are nearly ready to fledge, parents carry the fecal sacs away from the nest to detour predators. Bird diapers can be smelly!

NESTLING The gray downy chicks stay in the nest for 8–10 days. They begin to practice hopping when they are 8–11 days old.

FLEDGLING At 11–20 days of age, their feathers have grown in enough to begin flight lessons. At 20–30 days of age, the young can pick up food on their own.

JUVENILE At this age, teens practice escaping from predators by playing tag. They fatten up on insects before their long migration south.

Birding Tip

How close is too close? You are minding your wildlife manners when your presence does not change an animal's behavior. If an animal does notice you, move slowly and quietly away. Make a wildlife watching blind in your backyard with things you already have at home, such as old sheets or a tent. Camouflage your hideout and learn about your wild neighbors!

When

Ovenbirds are diurnal, active during the day and resting at night.

Migration

Spring Arrival: May
Fall Departure: September
Long-distance migrants. Immature and adult Ovenbirds migrate together at night 500–1000 feet in the air at 40 mph to wintering areas in South America.

Nesting

Begin nesting in mid- to late May with eggs hatching in early to mid-June in Minnesota. The nest is so well camouflaged it is nearly invisible! It looks like a Dutch oven, which gives this bird its name.

Getting Around

Ovenbirds walk on the ground and fly low to the ground. Watch for their tail to pump up and down when they fly from tree to tree.

Where to Look

Needs areas of deciduous and mixed deciduous-coniferous forests of at least 250 acres.
· Flandrau State Pk
· Tettegouche State Pk
· Itasca State Pk

Year-round	Summer
Migration	Winter

Deciduous Forest Habitat

White-breasted Nuthatch

Sitta carolinesis

Length: 6 inches
Wingspan: 11 inches

female

Females have a blue-gray cap and black on back of neck (nape)

Young look like female

Blue-gray back

Rusty brown undertail

Males have a black cap

Short, very strong black legs for holding onto tree bark and branches

White breast

Long, slightly curved bill tapers to a point

"Yank, yank, yank" means "I'm over here!" Both males and females use this call to check in with each other.

Look out below! I'm coming down headfirst!

The White-breasted Nuthatch has a game plan for finding food. It has to. There are other bird species after the same insect meal. The White-breasted Nuthatch is a "hop down the tree headfirst insect gleaner." They also hop up and to the side while looking for food. Where do they store their groceries? They cache the food in tree bark cracks. Pounding a sunflower seed into a bark crack can open the seed for eating right away or it can be covered with moss, rotten wood or snow for munching on later. A male nuthatch tried six different places in the bark and branches of a large maple tree to hide its yummy seed. Hidden that is, except from this author (alias wildlife detective)!

Habitat Café

Today's Special

white proso millet
BIRD FEEDER TREAT

Yumm . . . bring an order of grasshoppers, caterpillars, beetles, seeds and berries. White-breasted Nuthatches are omnivorous. Seeds provide fats and carbohydrates needed to refuel during winter months.

SPRING, SUMMER, FALL MENU:
Equal amounts of insects and seeds

WINTER MENU:
Mostly seeds and suet, less insects than during spring, summer and fall

Life Cycle

NEST The female builds the nest 5–20 feet above the ground in a rotted out tree knothole, tree cavity or even a nesting box. She brings in twigs and grasses for the nest base and lines it with fine grass, hair, fur, wool and feathers.

 EGGS About ½ inch long. The female incubates the clutch of 6–9 eggs for 11–12 days. The male enters the nesting hole only to feed the female.

MOM! DAD! Altricial. Mom and Dad make many trips for insects to feed their hungry brood. How many? Up to 22 trips per hour when the chicks are 19 days of age!

NESTLING The chicks stay in the nest for about 26 days.

FLEDGLING The young birds stay with their parents for a few weeks after they leave the nest.

JUVENILE Juveniles leave the territory where they were raised to find their own space.

Birding Tip

Mealworms for dinner! Birds that stay in Minnesota during the winter need protein to keep up their supply of heat-making energy. Take a trip to your local pet store or fishing bait shop and stock up on mealworms. Simply keep them in the refrigerator. (Ask your parents first—mealworms do not make the best pizza topping.) Place the worms in a flat bird feeder a few at a time and watch cardinals, nuthatches, juncos, jays, chickadees and woodpeckers chow down. Tasty!

When
White-breasted Nuthatches are diurnal. They feed during the day and rest at night.

Migration
Permanent resident. They stay all year and use their energy to find insects in the less crowded winter forest. Birds that migrate use their energy to make the long round-trip.

Nesting
Begin nest building in mid- to late April and lay their eggs in early May in Minnesota.

Getting Around
Nuthatches use their long, somewhat pointed wings for a quick darting flight from tree to tree. Because they have a short tail, they spread their feet far apart and at a slight angle from the tree bark for support while feeding. Watch them pick up a seed, fly off to a tree trunk, then hide the tidbit for a later snack.

Where to Look
Deciduous forests. Backyard trees, bird feeders, parks, orchards, farm woodlots with mature trees. Most of Minnesota except the very northeast where they may move farther south in harsh winters.

Year-round   Summer
Migration   Winter

Deciduous Forest Habitat

Downy Woodpecker

Picoides pubescens

Length: 6–7 inches
Wingspan: 12 inches

female

Males have red patch on nape (back of neck)

Females do not have red on nape (back of neck)

White belly

White stripe down the back

Young male has a red spot on top of his head

Black with white spotted wings

Black spots on white tail feathers

"Drum, drum" is rapped on dry limbs.

Built for the Job

Minnesota's most common and smallest woodpecker is designed to do its job of surviving very well. Downy Woodpeckers can balance on weed stems and small branches that the larger members of the woodpecker family cannot. Look for this black and white wonder balanced on the stems of goldenrod plants. They are most likely pecking wasp larvae from inside their cozy gall home. Using its strong bill, long barbed tongue (up to four times the length of its bill) and sticky spit, Downy Woodpeckers rake in insects from cracks and tunnels. Where does it store its long tongue? Curled inside its head like a tape measure!

Habitat Café

Today's Special

insect larvae in goldenrod galls

Yumm . . . bring an order of crickets, wasps, grasshoppers, ants, beetles, flies, spiders, acorns, berries and fruit. Downy Woodpeckers are omnivorous. Fill your feeders with suet, peanut butter and nuts.

SPRING, SUMMER, FALL, WINTER MENU:
Lots of insect larvae, some seeds

Life Cycle

NEST The female and male make the nesting hole in a tree, fencepost or tree stump 3–50 feet above the ground. The hole is 1¼ inches in diameter and 8–12 inches deep. They will use a birdhouse for roosting but not usually for nesting.

EGGS About ½ inch long. Both the male and female incubate the clutch of 4–5 eggs for 11–12 days.

MOM! DAD! Altricial. Mom and Dad put small, soft insects directly into the helpless chicks' open bills.

NESTLING By the time the young birds are nine days old, they climb to the top of the nest cavity to be fed and all the way to the entrance opening at 12 days of age. This makes Mom and Dad's job much easier!

FLEDGLING The young birds can fly and leave the nest at 18–22 days of age. They still depend on Mom and Dad for food for three weeks after leaving the nest.

JUVENILE The birds are mature enough to date, mate and raise their own young at one year of age.

Birding Tip

Make your own suet feeder. Suet is animal fat. In the wild, woodpeckers will eat the fat from a deer carcass. In town, you can buy beef suet at a grocery store. Place the suet in a mesh orange or onion bag, or pound it into the cracks of tree bark. With the help of an adult, melt suet over LOW heat. Place a string or length of yarn around the base of a pinecone and dip it into the melted suet. You can add millet, peanut hearts, and cornmeal. Hang your feeders outside on a tree limb.

When

Downy Woodpeckers are diurnal. They feed during the day and rest at night.

Migration

Permanent resident. Downy Woodpeckers stay in Minnesota all year.

Nesting

Downy Woodpeckers begin pairing up as early as October or November in Minnesota. Nesting begins in May.

Getting Around

How do they stay on a tree while drilling a hole or searching for insects? Zygodactyl means they have two toes pointing forward and two backward. Their long curved claws are super for getting a tight grip. Their stiff tail feathers act as a brace against the tree trunk. Look for a flash of white while the downy is in flight. The black barred tail has white outer feathers. Flight is undulating (up and down) in a series of wing flaps and then a bound forward.

Where to Look

Open deciduous woods of both old and new growth.
· City parks
· Backyard bird feeders
· Minnesota River Valley
   Birding Trail

Year-round	Summer
Migration	Winter

Deciduous Forest Habitat

Scarlet Tanager

Piranga olivacea

Length: 7 inches
Wingspan: 11–12 inches

female

Called the *Firebird*, males are bright scarlet red in the spring and summer; in winter, they wear the dull, camouflaged colors of the female

Females have brown wings and tail with a dull yellow belly and back

Black wings and tail

Young look like the female, but with black wings and back

"Chip-churr!"
The male sings this song to declare his territory.

Firebirds

Look to tall tree tops for fire-red male Scarlet Tanagers in Minnesota's large, deep deciduous forests. How large? Each nesting pair needs 4–8 acres for raising their young. Finding large, unbroken forests is not as easy as it once was. Explore St. Croix and Flandrau State Parks, Fond du Lac State Forest, Magney-Snively Park near Duluth, Rice Lake National Wildlife Refuge, and wooded areas along the Minnesota River for Tanagers. Watch for the yellow-olive females searching for food in the early morning and late afternoon. Come September, these forest specialists migrate long distances at night to the Neotropics. In the spring, the males return before the females to declare their territory.

Habitat Café

Today's Special

peanut butter with cornmeal
BIRD FEEDER TREAT

Yumm . . . bring an order of beetles, moths, caterpillars, ants, berries, cherries and grapes. Scarlet Tanagers are omnivorous. They catch protein-rich insects in trees and feed on summer fruits in Minnesota. In wintering areas, they eat mostly fruit.

SPRING, SUMMER, FALL MENU:
Mostly insects, some fruits and berries

WINTER MENU:
Mainly fruits, a few insects

Life Cycle

NEST The female builds the loose, saucer-shaped nest on a limb, 15–25 feet from the ground. Twigs and plant stalks are loosely woven to make the thin nest. A soft lining is made with fine grasses, rootlets and vine tendrils.

EGGS About ⅝ inch long. The female incubates the clutch of 3–5 eggs for 13–14 days. The male may bring her food.

MOM! DAD! Altricial. Chicks hatch with few downy feathers and orange skin so thin that their insides can be seen. Their eyes are closed. Both parents feed and care for the chicks.

NESTLING By the time they are 10 days of age, the chicks can fly short distances and are ready to leave the nest. That is a very BIG growth spurt!

FLEDGLING Fledgling chicks continue to be fed by their parents for the first two weeks they are out of the nest. After the two weeks and up until migration, they stay in the territory or live nearby.

JUVENILE At one year of age, tanagers can date, mate, nest and raise their own family.

Gross Factor

Chick Diapers: Keeping the nest clean is a chore for some bird parents. Fortunately, chicks defecate (poop) in tidy bags called fecal sacs. Like disposable diapers, fecal sacs have a strong outside liner to hold the poop. This liner is made up of edible sugars and proteins. The first few days, parents eat the fecal sacs! Does it make them sick? No. During the first days, the chicks do not produce harmful bacteria; once they do, Mom and Dad drop the diapers away from the nest.

When

Scarlet Tanagers are diurnal. They feed during the day and rest at night.

Migration

Spring Arrival: late May
Fall Departure: mid-Sept.
Long distance migrant to South and Central America, mainly Bolivia and Peru.

Nesting

Nest in mid- to late June in Minnesota's mature, unbroken hardwood and mixed forests. Need 4–8 acres of nesting territory for each pair of birds.

Getting Around

Scarlet Tanagers climb up and down on tree trunks, probing with their beaks for insects hidden in the bark. They will also hover and glean (pick up) for insects. These birds are strong fliers—good thing, too, because they have a long and nearly nonstop migration flight.

Where to Look

Mature oak forests of the St. Croix River Valley and the bottomland timber of the Mississippi River as far north as Itasca State Park.
· Inspiration Peak Wayside Pk

Year-round Migration	Summer Winter

Deciduous Forest Habitat

Eastern Bluebird

Sialia sialis

Length: 7 inches
Wingspan: 13 inches

Short, stout bill slightly notched at the tip for catching insects

Male is sky blue above

male and female

Young look like females but are speckled with blue wings

female

Females are duller in color than males

Rusty-orange throat and breast

White belly

"Tury, cherwee, cheye-ley." Male loudly sings this song to claim his territory. The same song is sung softly to tell the female on the nest, "Everything's O.K., dear."

Wildlife Hotel: Immediate Occupancy

Bluebirds need tree cavities for nesting. Some people view a rotting tree as useless and cut it down. A rotten tree is, in fact, a wildlife hotel complete with fast food and buffet dining areas. In 1977, some smart folks teamed up with the Minnesota DNR and the Audubon Chapter of Minneapolis Bluebird Recovery Committee. They built bluebird nesting boxes and placed them along forest edges and open rural and suburban areas that bluebirds need for catching insects. Since then, the number of Eastern Bluebirds in Minnesota has increased. You can become a part of this success story by planting and leaving valuable habitat, and building and monitoring your own bluebird nesting boxes.

Habitat Café

Yumm . . . bring an order of crickets, beetles, grasshoppers, ants, spiders, earthworms, snails and berries. Eastern Bluebirds are omnivorous. Put wiggly mealworms on the ground to invite a blue visitor. Most pet shops have mealworms.

SPRING, SUMMER, FALL MENU:
Lots of insects, some fruits and berries

WINTER MENU:
More fruits and berries than summer, but insects are still the main course

Today's Special
caterpillars

Life Cycle

NEST The female builds the nest cup of grasses in a natural tree cavity made by other birds such as woodpeckers, in tops of rotten fence posts and in nesting boxes.

EGGS About ⅝ inch long. The female incubates the clutch of 4–5 eggs for 12–14 days.

MOM! DAD! Altricial. Both Mom and Dad feed the young from their first hour until three weeks after they leave the nest.

NESTLING The gray downy chicks stay in the nest for 17–18 days. By 13 days of age, their feathers have grown in with male or female coloration.

FLEDGLING If you hear *Tu-a-wee*, near a nesting cavity or box you will know that a young bluebird is leaving the nest to perch on a nearby limb or in cover. They also give this call when they are waiting for their parents to feed them.

JUVENILE When the young bluebirds return in the spring, they are ready to date, mate, nest and raise their own young.

History Hangout

On March 21, 1901, Dr. Johan Hvoslef heard the first bluebird of the spring in Lanesboro, Minnesota. One hundred years later, March 23, 2001, Jim Gilbert of St. Peter, Minnesota, made note of the spring return of bluebirds to Minnesota. How do we know? They both kept phenology notes. Phenology is the study of the changing seasons. Be a part of history and keep your notes in the Journal Pages provided in the back of this book.

When

Eastern Bluebirds are diurnal. They feed during the day and rest at night.

Migration

Spring Arrival: March–April
Fall Departure: late October or early November
They migrate to the southeastern United States and Mexico.

Nesting

Eastern Bluebirds nest in Minnesota beginning in April–May. They raise 1–3 broods per summer.

Getting Around

Eastern Bluebirds sidle—they move sideways. They hop and walk sideways while turning halfway around. How does it scratch its head? By moving a foot up and over a drooping wing. They are true blue acrobats! Bluebirds fly low in open areas, about 10–12 feet above the ground. Their flight is higher on longer journeys.

Where to Look

Open habitats along deciduous forest edges.
· Eagle Bluff Env Learning Ctr
· Minnesota Landscape Arboretum

Year-round	Summer
Migration	Winter

Deciduous Forest Habitat

81

Baltimore Oriole

Icterus galbula

Length: 7–8 inches
Wingspan: 11–12 inches

female

Males are black with orange breast, underside and wing shoulder

Young look like female

Females are brown-olive on back and faded yellow underneath. Wings have a white wing bar.

One white wing bar

Orange-and-black tail

"Tee-dee-dee."
Nestlings:
"Bring food, more food!"

Dealing with Imposters

The buffalo that once roamed the open prairies were not alone. Brown-headed Cowbirds followed them, eating both insects they kicked up and insects living in the dung. Cowbirds didn't have time to stop and nest. Instead, they laid their eggs in the nests of birds that live where the prairie and forest meet. A female cowbird lays up to 40 eggs each year, none of which she raises. Baltimore Orioles are forest edge nesters and recipients of cowbird eggs. Cowbirds do not reimburse the host species for incubation, meals and around the clock chick-care. Baltimore Orioles have adapted a strategy in turn. They push the cowbird eggs out of the nest. Their plan in dealing with imposter eggs generally works.

Habitat Café

Today's Special

grape jelly and peas
BIRD FEEDER TREAT

Yumm . . . bring an order of caterpillars, grasshoppers, ants, beetles, bugs, spiders, blackberries, cherries, apples and raspberries. Fill a nectar feeder and watch for orioles in your backyard. Baltimore Orioles are omnivorous.

SPRING, SUMMER, FALL, WINTER MENU:
Mostly insects, some fruit

Life Cycle

NEST The female builds a pouch-like nest on the tip of a large tree branch. She hangs loops of plant fibers and long grass around the branch. Milkweed silk is woven through the loops to make a hanging basket 5–8 inches long. The pouch is lined with feathers and animal fur. Set out bright colored string, yarn or fabric strips in your yard and she may weave them into her hanging work of art!

EGGS About 1 inch long. The female incubates the clutch of 4–5 eggs for 12–14 days.

MOM! DAD! Altricial. Mom and Dad make about 13 trips per hour to feed their hungry chicks.

NESTLING The chicks stay in the nest for 12–13 days.

FLEDGLING When the young leave the nest, they can fly short distances. Mom and Dad bring the young birds food for two more weeks. They may take the kids to a nearby grape jelly feeder and stuff their beaks full of sticky jelly. Fresh green peas are popular, too.

JUVENILE In August, small flocks of juveniles group together and prepare for migration.

Did You Know?

In their Costa Rican wintering grounds, orioles feed on the fruit and insects found in both the tropical lowland forests and on coffee plantations. Planting Inga trees between the rows shades the coffee trees and makes more habitat for wildlife. Habitat is key. Well done, Costa Rica!

When

Baltimore Orioles are diurnal. They feed during the day and rest at night.

Migration

Spring Arrival: early May
Fall Departure: Aug.–Sept. Long-distance migrant south along the Mississippi Flyway to Mexico and then on to Central and South America.

Nesting

Baltimore Orioles begin nesting from mid- to late May in Minnesota.

Getting Around

Baltimore Orioles are strong fliers with powerful wing strokes. They hop from branch to branch to glean (pick up) insects. They can even hang upside down to eat fruit and weave their nests! This is a handy trick to know, because it can take the female Baltimore Oriole nearly a week to finish weaving the sock-like nest. That's a long time to hang upside-down!

Where to Look

Deciduous forests. Open woods and forest edges, parks, orchards and city neighborhoods where they can visit backyard oriole feeders.

Year-round Migration	Summer Winter

Deciduous Forest Habitat

Northern Cardinal

Cardinalis cardinalis

Length: 8–9 inches
Wingspan: 12 inches

female

Females are gray-tan with
pale red on crest and wings

Crest

Males are bright red

Red, conical bill
is shaped for
cracking open
hard seeds

Young look like female,
but with dark crest
and bill

"Chip, chip."
Male: "This is my territory."
"Took, took."
Female: "All clear. You
can bring the food to
the nest now."

Newcomer to Minnesota

Northern Cardinals are fairly new to Minnesota. They arrived here in the late 1800s from states in the southeast. The first Minnesota record was in Minneapolis, October 23, 1875. What conditions brought these brilliant birds north? Northern Cardinals can live in different kinds of shrubby areas away from people or right in their backyards. They need enough food and low shrubs and trees to nest in and raise their young. With the opening of forest edges and the creation of shrubby and semi-open areas, cardinals are adding to their range in Minnesota. Cardinals are moving north to Brainerd and even as far as the North Shore of Lake Superior near Duluth. Welcome!

Habitat Café

Yumm . . . bring an order of grasshoppers, cicadas, beetles, butterflies, moths, seeds and fruit. Cardinals are omnivorous. When the trees leaf out, they feed on leaf buds and insect larvae. In the fall, they eat seeds and fruit. Young chicks eat protein-rich insects.

SPRING, SUMMER, FALL MENU:
Insects are the main course, with hearty helpings of seeds and fruits

WINTER MENU:
Mainly seeds and fruits, some insects

Life Cycle

NEST The female builds the bowl-shaped nest in a thick tangle of shrubs or in a small tree within 10 feet of the ground. Using her bill, the female chews the twigs to make them easier to bend around her body. Then, sitting in the center of the nest and turning around, she pushes out with her feet against the twigs, grapevine bark, leaves or weed stems to form a cup. The nest is lined with fine grass.

EGGS About ⅞ inch long. The female incubates 2–3 eggs for 11–13 days. The male brings her food.

MOM! DAD! Altricial. Mom and Dad both care for the chicks.

NESTLING The gray downy chicks stay in the nest for 8–10 days while their feathers grow in.

FLEDGLING When young cardinals leave the nest at 9–12 days of age, they have small crests on their heads. Even though they can fly a short distance, they usually perch on the same branch for the first 11 days while their parents bring food.

JUVENILE At one year of age, the young can sing an adult song, date, mate, and raise their own young.

Unsolved Mystery

Why do some songbirds rub or hold ants on their feathers and skin? Why does a bird lay on an anthill and allow ants to crawl into its feathers? Biologists have not solved the mystery of this behavior, called anting. Ideas include: ants have an acid that protects birds against parasites, fungus and bacteria that could harm their feathers; it soothes their skin during feather molting; they store ants for eating later; and/or the ants' acid works to ready food for eating. Get antsy and solve the mystery!

When

Northern Cardinals are diurnal. They feed during the day and rest at night.

Migration

Permanent residents. To stay warm during Minnesota's cold winters, it fluffs out its feathers to trap body heat and tucks its bill inside its wing.

Nesting

Northern Cardinals begin nesting in May in Minnesota. They raise 1–2 broods per season.

Getting Around

Northern Cardinals hop on the ground and take short flights from branch to branch when looking for insects and buds to eat. They clean and sharpen their bill by rubbing the edges of on something hard. On winter afternoons, they often become active before sunset, looking for a snack before they go to sleep.

Where to Look

Southern half of Minnesota. Thick, shrubby areas of deciduous forests, farm windbreaks, urban woodlots and backyards.
· Minnesota River Valley Birding Trail
· Root River State Trail
· Great River Birding Trail

Year-round	Summer
Migration	Winter

Deciduous Forest Habitat

Purple Martin

Progne subis

Length: 8 inches
Wingspan: 18 inches

The short, wide beak opens large to catch insects while flying

Long, pointed wings of a swallow

Males are glossy blue-black all over

colony nest box

female

Females have a blue-black back and are gray and white below. They have a gray and brown collar at the back of their neck.

Juvenile looks like female with a gray forehead

Forked tail

"Cher, cher."
Males and females may shake their body and flap their wings while giving this year-round call.

There's No Place Like Home

"Is anyone home?" Over one hundred years ago Purple Martins made this call into old woodpecker tree holes as they scouted for a place to nest. They weren't the only ones. House Sparrows and European Starlings, both bird species brought into the United States from Europe, were moving into the holes without even a courtesy knock at the door. They were replacing Purple Martins in their natural woodland habitat. That is, until people in Minnesota began building. By 1900, Purple Martins were nesting almost entirely in colony nest boxes. Martins can be very sociable neighbors. When Purple Martins move into your Minnesota neighborhood there will be fewer insects to pester you. Start building!

Habitat Café

Yumm . . . bring an order of crane flies, moths, butterflies, dragonflies and all other flying insects! Purple Martins are insectivores. When cold, wet weather lasts for more than 3–4 days and insects are not flying, Purple Martins can get very hungry indeed. If it lasts for too long, it can be dangerous for martins.

SPRING, SUMMER, FALL, WINTER MENU:
Entirely insects

Life Cycle

NEST The female builds the nest inside a nesting box, a gourd house, natural tree cavity, woodpecker hole or among rock piles. She uses weeds, straw, grasses and feathers. Mud may support the edges.

EGGS About ⅝ inch long. The female incubates the clutch of 4–6 eggs for 15–18 days.

MOM! DAD! Altricial. Both Mom and Dad feed the young and do diaper duty (remove fecal sacs).

NESTLING Feathers do not start to break through their thin skin until they are 12 days old. When growth starts, it is fast.

FLEDGLING At 28–29 days old, flight feathers are grown in. They are coaxed out of the nest by their parents and led away from the nesting colony.

JUVENILE At 7–10 days out of the nest, they can catch insects. Juveniles group together in late summer and prepare for migration. On their spring return they are able to date, mate and raise their own young.

Unsolved Mystery

Before people began building apartment-style nest boxes, did martins nest together in colonies? Here are a few clues: Native Americans in Florida and North and South Carolina made nesting gourds for Purple Martins as early as 1712. Early Minnesota records of Purple Martins include a sighting in Central Minnesota in 1870 and nests found among large rocks on Spirit and Hennepin Islands in Mille Lacs Lake in 1886.

When

Purple Martins are diurnal. They feed during the day and rest at night.

Migration

Spring Arrival: mid-April
Fall Departure: Aug.–Sept.
Long-distance migrant in large flocks to South America. Will form massive wintering colonies in Brazil.

Nesting

Purple Martins begin nest building in May and lay their eggs in June in Minnesota.

Getting Around

Purple Martins are sssswift! They feed at heights of 15–45 feet. When chasing insect prey, they make sudden turns, speed, then spread their forked tail (brakes) and catch the insect. How do they take a bath and cool off? They skim the surface of the water and soak their belly feathers. Females go back to the nest and provide "air conditioning" to the young.

Where to Look

You can find Purple Martins all over the state. They are often seen in open areas near water, and around boulder crevices, bridges and colony nest boxes.

Year-round	Summer
Migration	Winter

Deciduous Forest Habitat

American Robin

Turdus migratorius

Length: 9–11 inches
Wingspan: 15–16 inches

Gray above with very dark head, wings and tail

White eye-ring and white chin

female

Females not as brightly colored as males

In flight, look for the white between their tummy and tail

"Red" breast—brown to dark red-orange

Young have speckled breast and white flecks on their dark backs

White tips on outer tail feathers

Brown legs

"Cheerily, cheer-up, cheer-up, cheer-up, cheerily, cheer-up!" This cheery song is sung during the time of nesting and incubation.

Squirmy Worms & Super-sized Storage

When you spy a robin with its head turned to the side and looking with one eye at the ground, it is probably ready to pounce on an insect with its yellow bill. Rather than eat it right away, the robin may store the food in its stretchy esophagus to digest later. Robins eat about 14 feet of earthworms in one day. At this rate, how many feet of earthworms could a robin eat in a week? Do the math! In the winter, robins pack their esophagus full of berries before the sun goes down. They digest food from this storage space when their body needs a snack before morning. Delicious!

Habitat Café

Yumm . . . bring an order of earthworms, beetles, grasshoppers, larvae, crickets, spiders, berries and other fruits. American Robins are omnivorous. They need more protein rich-insects during egg-laying and molting season than in the winter.

SPRING, SUMMER, FALL MENU:
Mostly fruit and berries, lots of insects

WINTER MENU:
Mainly fruit and berries, some insects

Life Cycle

NEST The female builds the nest in the fork of a tree, on a fence post, a window ledge or a manmade nesting platform. The outside of the nest is made with dead grass and twigs. To get just the right shape, she uses the bend of her wing to press from the inside. Next, she carries mud in her bill for the inside. She turns her body in the hollow of the cup for the final fitting. The nest is lined with soft, dead grass.

EGGS About 1 inch long. The female incubates the clutch of 3–4 bright blue eggs for 12–14 days.

MOM! DAD! Altricial. The chicks hatch without feathers. Their skin is so thin that the inside of their tiny bodies can be seen.

NESTLING The chick that begs the soonest, stretches its neck the highest and holds it beak closest to the parent gets food FIRST. During the first 10 days, each nestling gets 35–40 feedings per day.

FLEDGLING They leave the nest at 13 days of age and stay on the ground, fed mostly by Dad while Mom gets ready for the next brood. Leave young robins for their parents to care for. Keep your cat inside.

JUVENILE In late August, juveniles form a flock and prepare to migrate south.

Birding Tip

Make a small mud puddle in your backyard. (It's a good idea to ask first.) Watch from afar as a female robin takes mud for building her nest. When you see a mud-covered female, you'll know her nest is nearby. Set out bright colored yarn and string. She may use this in her nest, too!

When

American Robins are diurnal. They feed during the day and rest at night.

Migration

Spring Arrival: late March–April
Fall Departure: late Sept.–Oct. Short distance migrant. Winters in southeastern states in areas without snow cover and plenty of food such as fruit from shrubs.

Nesting

American Robins begin nesting in Minnesota in mid-April. They raise one or two broods each year.

Getting Around

Robins are speedy, using their sturdy leg muscles to run and hop in the grass. You may see them stop and look around quickly for prey or predators, and then they are off and running again. During migration, robins are fast, straight fliers with their pointed wings (20–36 mph). They use their medium-length tail for steering through trees during a quick escape.

Where to Look

Most of Minnesota in areas with open woods, forest edges, farm windbreaks, parks, backyards.
· A *Super Adaptor*

Year-round	Summer
Migration	Winter

American Woodcock

Scolopax minor

Length: 11 inches
Wingspan: 18 inches

female brooding chicks

Long bill is extra sensitive to help find earthworms and soil insects

Short neck

Disguised in leaf brown and dead grass feather pattern

Juveniles look like dully colored adults. They may have a dark gray band on their throat

Short legs

Male and female look alike

Whistling Wings: The sharp whistling comes from air rushing through the three narrow and stiff outer wing feathers.

Romance in the Skies

Romance in the skies requires low light. Go to an open field near the Minnesota or Mississippi River in April to early May when the faint light of dawn, dusk or moonlight casts only a whisper of your shadow—shh. Listen for the winged notes of the American Woodcock as he spirals to the moon and flutters to earth in an aerial dance. He shows off his desire for a nearby female as he struts on the short grass. Tail up and spread, he makes a peenting sound (buzz) every few seconds. Suddenly he rises, flying off at an angle in whistling circles ever higher until he reaches 200–300 feet. Like a falling star, he flickers down through the sky landing where he started to repeat his ballad.

Habitat Café

Yumm . . . bring an order of earthworms with a side of larvae, ants, slugs and snails. American Woodcocks are insectivores. They glean (pick up) insects with their long 2½-inch bill. Eyes are far back on head so they can see while bill is deep in the ground.

SPRING, SUMMER, FALL MENU:
≈ Lots of earthworms, some insects and snails

WINTER MENU:
≈ More insects and snails than summer, but still mostly earthworms

Life Cycle

NEST The simple ground nest is a slight depression in the leaves. The female may line the rim of the nest with a few twigs.

EGGS About 1⅛ inches long. The female incubates the clutch of 4 eggs for 20–21 days. If the female is flushed from the nest during incubation, she may not return to it. Respect the needs of wildlife.

MOM! DAD! Precocial. The young chicks leave the nest as soon as they hatch. If in danger, they "freeze." Mom feeds the chicks for the first week. Then the young probe for earthworms and insects on their own. They are able to fly at 18 days of age.

JUVENILE Juvenile woodcocks set out on their own at 4–5 weeks of age. They join with others on fields at night until fall migration. In Minnesota, American Woodcock migration may be as early as September or as late as November.

Did You Know?

A woodcock's bill is designed for pulling worms from the soil. The tips of the mandible can be moved apart while the base of the bill is held together (like a pair of pinchers or tweezers). Stick your pencil in the mud and pull it out. The hole will look like one made by a woodcock. Finding "pencil holes" as you explore Minnesota's damp river forests is a clue that a woodcock may be near! You might also want to do a little research about the woodcock's upside-down brain!

When
Crepuscular. They are active near sunrise and sunset when the light is dim. May feed in day.

Migration
Spring Arrival: March–early May
Fall Departure: late September
Short-distance migrant. Migrate by night, low to the ground in small flocks to southern U.S.

Nesting
American Woodcocks nest in woody areas near rivers in Minnesota during May.

Getting Around
American Woodcocks walk along the ground with their long bill ahead of them clearing leaves out of the way. Look for slender tracks in soft mud with 3 toes forward and 1 short toe backward (1½–2 inches long/wide). They can swim short distances. They fly low to the ground in a zig-zag to avoid capture by predators. Try zig-zag running during recess to keep away from friends trying to "capture" you!

Where to Look
· Open areas with trees/shrubs near a river.
· Blue Mounds State Pk
· Roseau River Wildlife Mgmt Area
· Whitewater Wildlife Mgmt Area
· Minneopa State Pk

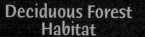

Year-round	Summer
Migration	Winter

Deciduous Forest Habitat

Brown Thrasher

Toxostoma rufum

Length: 11–12 inches
Wingspan: 13 inches

Yellow eye

Immature thrashers look similar to the adults but with gray eyes and cream-colored spotting on the upper sides of their bodies

Long, slightly curved bill used as a broom to sweep leaves aside and pick up insects

Rusty colored upper body

Rusty colored, long tail

White underside with streaks of dark brown

Males and females look alike

The male's spring song declares his space and desire for a female.

Beethoven of the Forest

If ever a bird were a composer, it is the Brown Thrasher. Singing from a perch with his tail to the ground, the male sings a catchy tune. The song has double phrases with little start or end. Brown Thrashers are a woodland orchestra, singing more than one note at a time and each note at a different intensity. A bird's voice box, or syrinx, has two chambers, allowing a bird to duet with itself. This can make different tones at the same time. Birds do not have vocal cords. They control volume by air sacs, which inflate to put pressure on the muscles of the syrinx. This makes a range of different sounds. Brown Thrashers compose songs from 1,000 different musical phrases.

Habitat Café

Today's Special
peanuts and mealworms
BIRD FEEDER TREAT

Yumm . . . bring an order of grasshoppers, ants, beetles, acorns and berries. Brown Thrashers are omnivorous. They eat plant and animal matter, depending on the season.

SPRING, SUMMER, FALL MENU:
   Mainly insects, lots of berries and fruit

WINTER MENU:
   Less berries and more insects than spring, summer and fall

Life Cycle

NEST The female and male build the twig basket nest 2–5 feet above the ground in the fork of a tree or shrub. At times they will nest on the ground. The basket nest is made in four steps, beginning with a bulky base of twigs and vines woven together, followed by a layer of leaves, and then a layer of small roots, stems and twigs. Lastly, the nest is lined with small grass rootlets that they clean by stomping (thrashing) the dirt off with their feet. A very clean and cozy nest!

EGGS About 1 inch long. The female and male both incubate the clutch of 3–5 eggs for 11–12 days.

MOM! DAD! Altricial. Both parents feed and care for the quickly growing young. In just 9 days the chicks have their feathers.

NESTLING The downy chicks stay in the nest for 11–12 days.

FLEDGLING Parents stay with the young until they are 28–30 days old. Gradually, the parents bring less and less food as the young become more independent.

JUVENILE They are ready to date, mate and raise their own young when spring comes around.

Did You Know?

Listen for the repeating phrases for a sure clue that you are tapping in time to the Beethoven of the forest. "Plant-a-seed, plant-a-seed, bury-it, bury-it, cover-it-up, cover-it-up, let-it-grow, let-it-grow, pull-it-up, pull-it-up, eat-it, eat-it, yum-yum, yum-yum." Do Brown Thrashers sing these words? No, people give words to bird sounds to help them remember and identify them. Trek to the woods to listen to their song firsthand and compose your own phrases. Be creative!

When

Brown Thrashers are diurnal, active during the day and resting at night.

Migration

Spring Arrival: early to mid-April
Fall Departure: Sept.–Oct.
They are short-distance migrants moving to the southern United States in the winter, preferring areas that stay above freezing (+32 degrees F). Some may remain in southern Minnesota during mild winters, where they feed on berries and tree fruits.

Nesting

In Minnesota, Brown Thrashers build their nests in May and lay their eggs in May and June.

Getting Around

Brown Thrashers spend most of their time on the ground walking and running after insects and hopping over brush and small trees. Their flight is low to the ground from shrub to shrub. Long, heavy legs are built to kick up leaves from the forest floor.

Where to Look

Shrubby, deciduous forest edges, wooded fencerows, farm windbreaks and wooded parks with open areas for finding tasty insects to feed upon.

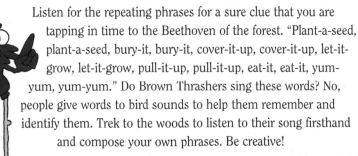

Year-round	Summer
Migration	Winter

Deciduous Forest Habitat

Mourning Dove

Zenaida macroura

Length: 11–13 inches
Wingspan: 18 inches

side profile

Dark brown eyes with an edge of blue skin; one black spot below.

Small head with a bluish crown

Males have rosy colored breast

Light gray above and buff below with black spot on wing and tail

Females have a tan breast and brown crown and are smaller than males

Short, red legs and fleshy red feet

Young are mottled with white wing tips

"Coo-oo, OO-OO-OO." The male's call to attract a female. Try this. Blow softly across the neck of an open bottle. It will sound similar to a dove.

Long tail that comes to a point

Cooing All Over Minnesota

Coo-oooo-oo-oo... You may wake up to the soothing coos of a love-struck Mourning Dove in St. Paul, Bemidji or Blue Earth. You may hear the whistle of their wings on a farm near Preston or farther northwest near Wheaton. Word has it, they have even been heard near Lake Wobegon. Mourning Doves are *Super Adaptors*, able to live in many different habitats all over Minnesota. As long as they can find seeds to eat and cover to nest in, Mourning Doves will be in our cities, farms, parks and suburban neighborhoods. Spread cracked corn on the ground. A cooing neighbor may come close enough to sketch, photograph or to simply enjoy their coo...mpany.

Habitat Café

Yumm . . . bring an order of seeds. Mourning Doves are herbivores. They eat seeds scattered over short grass and from bird feeders with a perch. At times, they will eat insects.

SPRING, SUMMER, FALL, WINTER MENU:
Almost all seeds

Life Cycle

NEST The nest is built in a tree or shrub, in an old nest of another bird such as a robin, on the ledge of a building or on the ground. Both parents make the flimsy platform nest of twigs lined with finer twigs.

EGGS About ⅞ inch long. For 14–15 days. Dad incubates the 2 eggs during the day and Mom takes the night shift.

MOM! DAD! Altricial. For the first 4–6 days, Mom and Dad feed the young crop milk. This bird baby formula is a secretion from their crop that has protein, water, fat and minerals. Seeds are gradually added to the crop milk at an increasing rate each day until the young are able to eat seeds on their own.

NESTLING At least one parent stays at the nest at all times.

FLEDGLING Young leave the nest at 15 days of age. They continue to be fed seeds by Dad in decreasing amounts until they are 30 days old when they can forage for seed on their own. Mom is busy getting ready for another brood.

JUVENILE Juveniles group with other immature doves and move to areas with plentiful food, such as harvested wheat.

Did You Know?

Mourning Doves pick up as many seeds from the ground as their bi-lobed crop will hold. The seeds are digested later in the safety of their nesting and roosting site. A bird's crop is a large sac at the bottom of the esophagus. How many seeds can a Mourning Dove's crop hold? The highest number recorded was over 17,200 annual bluegrass seeds!

When

Mourning Doves are diurnal. They feed during the day and rest at night.

Migration

Spring Arrival: March–April
Fall Departure: October
Long distance migrant to central and southern regions of the U.S. Some travel as far as Mexico and Costa Rica. During mild winters, some stay in central and southern Minnesota.

Nesting

Mourning Doves begin nesting in Minnesota in April and continue until August. Raise 1–2 broods per year.

Getting Around

Mourning Doves walk or run on the ground when foraging for food rather than hopping. They move south in the cold months because their fleshy feet are easily frostbitten. In flight, Mourning Doves are swift, changing direction and height quickly.

Where to Look

All of Minnesota, except the northern coniferous forests and deep, thick deciduous forests. Your neighborhood!
· A *Super Adaptor*

Year-round	Summer
Migration	Winter

Deciduous Forest Habitat

Cooper's Hawk

Accipiter cooperii

Length: 15–19 inches
Wingspan: 27–37 inches

soaring

Red eyes

juvenile

Short, rounded
wings for cruising
around trees

**Immature: Yellow eyes.
Brown back with brown
bars below.**

Gray above;
underside is
white with rust-
colored bars

Females are ⅓ larger
than the males

"Cak-cak-cak!"
This call is given by
males and females when
the nest is in danger or
the bird is excited.

Long gray tail
with black
bands and a
white tip

Small Birds Beware–Accipiter in the Area!

Cooper's Hawks have eyes so large there is little room left in their skull to move them. A bony eyebrow shield protects them. Hawks move their entire head from side to side, and up and down to get a full range of vision. They are equipped with a monocle, a pair of binoculars and a telescope! Monocular vision allows each eye to see a separate image. The bird can scan and search for prey. Once located, binocular vision (both eyes seeing forward) allows the bird to judge the distance and depth of moving prey. Telescope vision then allows the hawk to zero in on prey by making the image larger. Small birds beware—a Cooper's Hawk with eyes nearly as big as its stomach may be spying on you!

Habitat Café

Today's Special
bats

Yumm . . . bring an order of Mourning Doves, robins, Blue Jays, starlings, chipmunks, rabbits, squirrels and mice with a side of frog. Cooper's Hawks are carnivorous. During nesting season, prey may be cached in a roost tree.

SPRING, SUMMER, FALL, WINTER MENU:
Mainly birds, with a few mammals, reptiles, amphibians and insects

Life Cycle

NEST The male and female build the bulky twig and stick nest 20–60 feet high in a deciduous or coniferous tree. The 2-foot-wide nest is lined with small chips or flakes of bark.

EGGS About 1½ inches long. The female incubates the clutch of 4–5 eggs for 24–36 days.

MOM! DAD! Altricial. Mom broods the young for the first two weeks. She spreads her wings as a rain or sun umbrella.

NESTLING Dad brings the food and Mom tears the prey into bite-sized pieces. Parents carry away food pellets and uneaten food. Diaper duty? Not in this nest. The young are able to scoot to the rim of the nest and take care of this stinky job on their own.

FLEDGLING The young can fly and leave the nest when they are 30 days old to roost nearby. Mom and Dad continue to bring food for seven more weeks.

JUVENILE At two years of age they are ready to date, mate and raise their own young.

Do the Math

In a study of a Cooper's Hawk nest, researchers found that it took an average of 66 robin-sized prey to raise one young hawk to the age of six weeks. How many prey would parent hawks need to capture for a family of three chicks over six weeks? Four chicks? Five chicks? Where do they find prey? Watch your bird feeders. Cooper's Hawks will come to bird feeders. Answer on pages 194-195.

When

Cooper's Hawks are diurnal. They feed during the day and rest at night.

Migration

Spring Arrival: mid-March–April
Fall Departure: Sept.–Oct.
Short- to long-distant migrants to the southern United States, Mexico and Central America.

Nesting

Cooper's Hawks begin nesting in May in Minnesota.

Getting Around

Cooper's Hawks fly low to the ground, darting and dodging through trees in a series of fast wing beats and then a swift glide. Gliding saves energy, using only $\frac{1}{20}$ of that used in wing flapping flight. Using surprise attacks, it pounces on prey with sharp talons, holds prey with both feet tucked close to its body and flies to its nest or roost tree. Lunch is served.

Where to Look

Deciduous and mixed deciduous-coniferous forests, often near a river or lake. They hunt along forested edges.
· Minnesota River Valley Birding Trail
· Great River Birding Trail

Year-round Migration	Summer Winter

Deciduous Forest Habitat

Pileated Woodpecker

Dryocopus pileatus

Length: 16–19 inches
Wingspan: 29 inches

feeding young

female

Zebra-striped cheeks; males have a red mustache under their bill

The male raises his red crest to look bigger when defending his area, or to look "cool" for a female

Female has a red crest. She does not have a red mustache or forehead.

Strong feet have two toes facing forward and two facing backward for grasping and balancing

"DRUM, DRUM drum, drum."
Male: "This is my territory, males stay away. Females welcome!"

There's No Place Like Home

To a pair of Pileated Woodpeckers there's no place like their home territory, all 150–200 acres. In Minnesota, these old growth, thick, forested areas are found along rivers and lakes. Chiseling in a large, soft tree of at least 16 inches in diameter (thickness of the trunk), Pileated Woodpeckers make 1–16 holes. Do they use all the holes? Rarely. Extra holes are used by forest mammals, reptiles and amphibians for safe, warm places to sleep and nest. Bird buddies include House Wrens and Downy, Hairy and Red-bellied Woodpeckers. In coniferous forests, Red-breasted Nuthatches and Northern Saw-whet Owls owe a chirp of thanks to the largest woodpecker in the neighborhood.

Habitat Café

Yumm . . . bring an order of carpenter ants and wood boring beetles and larvae with a side order of wild berries, nuts and suet. Pileated Woodpeckers are omnivorous. They use their very sticky, forked tongue to spear insects. Look for tree holes up to two feet long for a clue that this large woodpecker has been in the area for lunch.

SPRING, SUMMER, FALL, WINTER MENU: Lots of insects, some seeds

Life Cycle

NEST Each year the male and female bore a new nesting hole 15–70 feet above the ground in a soft, deciduous or coniferous tree. The entrance hole is 3¼ inch wide by 3½ inches long and 1–2 feet deep.

EGGS About 1¼ inches long. Both the female and male incubate the clutch of 3–4 eggs for 15–18 days. Dad incubates at night and Mom during the day.

MOM! DAD! Altricial. Hatch naked, unable to see and with the remains of the yolk sac still attached to their belly. Both parents bring regurgitated insects until the chicks are able to digest whole insects.

NESTLING Feathers begin at 10–16 days of age. At 15 days, the young peek out of the entrance hole with a "chrr—chrr" call when they see their parents.

FLEDGLING At 22–26 days, the young leave the nest, flying nearly 100 yards without any warm-up or practice!

JUVENILE For the next several months, the young are fed a few meals by their parents. They leave in the fall and find their own territory to date, mate, nest and raise their own young in the spring.

Do the Math

How many drumbeats can a woodpecker drum? Do the math. If they make 15 drumbeats in one series and a series is repeated five times in a row every 60 seconds, how many drumbeats can a woodpecker drum in ten minutes? How do they make ____(your answer here) drumbeats without getting a BIG headache? Shock absorbers. Strong neck muscles and an extra-thick skull help cushion the brain. Answer on pages 194-195.

When

Pileated Woodpeckers are diurnal, active during the day and resting at night.

Migration

Permanent resident. Pileated Woodpeckers remain in their breeding territory all year.

Nesting

Minnesota's largest woodpecker needs 150–200 acres of mature forest for nesting and breeding territory per pair. Egg laying and incubation begin in May in Minnesota. Listen for their courtship drumming—they will even use telephone poles!

Getting Around

Watch for their white wing patches that flash in a slow but high-energy flight of gliding and quick wing-strokes. Pileated Woodpeckers climb up trunks with the use of their strong feet and stiff, supportive tail.

Where to Look

Minnesota's deciduous and coniferous old growth forests and heavily forested areas along rivers and lakes.
· Lake Shetek State Pk
· Flandrau State Pk
· Tettegouche State Pk
· Rice Lake Nat'l Wildlife Refuge
· Woldsfeld Woods
        · Carver Park Reserve

Year-round Migration	Summer Winter

Deciduous Forest Habitat

Barred Owl

Strix varia

Length: 17–24 inches
Wingspan: 4½–5 feet

landing

Yellow beak

Dark blue eyes surrounded by facial disc that looks like huge glasses

Gray-brown with bars across its breast

Brown downward streaks on the pale belly

Females and males look alike with females generally larger.

Young look like the adults

"Who cooks for you, who cooks for you all?" Most common in February—early March in Minnesota.

Of Friend and Foe

Barred Owls and Red-shouldered Hawks hang out in the same habitat. They have an understanding. This is not the case between Barred Owls and Great Horned Owls. In small forest spaces and broken-up forests, Barred Owls move out when Great Horned Owls move in. Why? Great Horned Owls kill Barred Owls. They kill the young Barred Owls in the nest, young that have just left the nest and even adults. In larger forested areas, all is well. Each species has enough space to spread out between their territories and there is a greater supply of food. Friend or foe? Habitat is the key.

Habitat Café

Today's Special
mice

Yumm . . . bring an order of small mammals, a few small birds, and a couple reptiles and amphibians. Barred Owls are carnivorous. They will hang around bird feeders to catch the mice and voles that are attracted to fallen seed on the ground.

SPRING, SUMMER, FALL, WINTER MENU:
Mostly mammals, some birds, reptiles, amphibians and insects

Life Cycle

NEST Barred Owls use a hollow tree cavity or an old hawk, crow, heron or squirrel nest in the top of a tall tree. The recycled nest may be lined with some of their own feathers. They will also use a nesting box.

EGGS About 1⅞ inches long. The female incubates the clutch of 2–3 eggs for 28–33 days.

MOM! DAD! Altricial. As soon as they hatch, the white fuzz balls call and beg for food. Dad hunts and Mom tears the food into soft bite-sized pieces. She stays at the nest for most of the first two weeks, warming the chicks until their larger feathers grow in.

NESTLING Starting after the third week, Dad leaves prey in the nest while Mom is gone. They learn to tear apart their own dinner.

FLEDGLING The young leave the nest still unable to fly when they are 4–5 weeks old and perch on a branch as they wait for Mom and Dad to bring food. Flying lessons begin when they are 10 weeks of age.

JUVENILE Mom and Dad bring food until early fall, when the teens move away to establish their own spaces. They are mature enough to date, mate and raise their own young when they are 2 years old.

Did You Know?

Our ears do not hear the full range of sounds that birds make. How do we know? We can see the bird sounds that we hear and don't hear on an electric sonogram. When you hear an echo in the forest darkness that sounds like monsters gone mad, this is a pair of Barred Owls "jiving" a duet of hoots, caws, cackles and gurgles. All this ruckus to impress and bond to each other. Of course, they sleep during the day!

When

Nocturnal, active during the night and resting during the day. Hunting is done mostly right after dark and just before dawn.

Migration

Permanent resident: Barred Owls live all year in Minnesota.

Nesting

Barred Owls are early nesters. They begin to nest and lay eggs in March–April.

Getting Around

Barred Owls perch in trees to listen and watch for movement of prey below. Once alerted to prey, the owl drops like a bullet on silent wings to snatch its target. They have paths they use routinely through their territory.

Where to Look

Mature (older) deciduous and mixed deciduous-coniferous forests often near a river or lake.
· Beltrami State Forest
· Itasca State Pk
· Manomin Pk
· MN River Valley Nat'l Wildlife Refuge (NWR)
· St. Croix Wild River State Pk
· Whitewater Wildlife Mgmt Area
· Minneopa State Pk
· Roseau River Wildlife Mgmt Area
· Rydell River Wildlife Mgmt Area
· Tamarac NWR
         · Forestville State Pk
         · Rice Lake NWR

Year-round	Summer
Migration	Winter

Great Horned Owl

Bubo virginianus

Length: 18–25 inches
Wingspan: 3–5 feet

in flight

Very large, yellow eyes

Ear tufts. Only large Minnesota owl with long, feathered ear tufts.

Hooked beak to tear the muscles and bones of prey

Facial disc of feathers funnel sound waves to their ears for extraordinary hearing

Both males and females have brown, black and cream lines over most of their body with a white bib

Females are heavier and larger than males

"Who-hoo-ho-oo?" or, "This is my territory." Hooting duets between paired males and females can be heard from January until the first eggs are laid.

Flying Mousetrap

Tucked under your winter covers or wrapped in summer's heat with fireflies lighting your room, the hooting of Great Horned Owls can wake you just about anywhere in Minnesota. Winter is the best time to listen for owls. However, I've been driven to giggles on summer nights listening to young owls practicing their who-whos. *Super Adaptors*, they live in cities, rural farming areas and places in between. They need a large tree for nesting and plenty of mice, rabbits, squirrels and skunks for the taking. The full menu includes stray cats and animals as large as a porcupine! Hear a Great Horned Owl in the night and know that this flying mousetrap is hard at work in your neighborhood.

Habitat Café

Today's Special
pet cats—
keep "Kitty"
indoors!

Yumm . . . bring an order of mice, rabbits, hares, ground squirrels, muskrats, squirrels, pocket gophers, snakes, small birds, pheasants, ducks and geese. They may take animals as large as a raccoon, skunk, porcupine or Great Blue Heron. Great Horned Owls are carnivorous.

SPRING, SUMMER, FALL, WINTER MENU: Mostly mammals, a few birds

Life Cycle

NEST These big owls do not make their own nest. They use a hollow tree cavity or an old hawk, crow, heron or squirrel nest in the top of a tall tree. Owls may line the recycled nest with some of their own feathers.

EGGS About 1⅞ inches long. The female incubates the clutch of 2–3 eggs for 28–33 days. She does not leave the eggs for more than a few minutes at a time to keep them from freezing.

MOM! DAD! Altricial. Cold, wind and snow calls for Mom to brood the young downy chicks for the first three weeks. Dad brings food. As feathers replace their down, Mom, too, leaves to hunt.

NESTLING Able to feed themselves at 20–27 days of age.

FLEDGLING At six weeks of age, young owls venture out to nearby branches. Their first test flights begin the following week.

JUVENILE Teenage owls stay with their parents during the summer and set out to find their own territories in late fall and early winter. At two years of age, they are able to mate and raise their own young.

Gross Factor

What does an owl do with the bones and fur of their eaten prey? Forms them into a pellet and spits them back up. You'll know you're under an owl roost when you find gray, 2–3 inch pellets. Break open a compact pellet and you may discover the tiny bones of a mouse, the jawbone of a rabbit, spine sections of a gopher and the beak of a starling, all surrounded by undigested fur. WOW!

When

Nocturnal. Feed at night and rest during the day. At times, they will hunt during the day.

Migration

Permanent resident. Stay all year in Minnesota. With many other predators having flown south for the winter, they take advantage of less competition for the small mammals that scurry on and under the snow.

Nesting

Minnesota's earliest nesting bird, they begin nesting in February. This is an adaptation to provide for the long time it takes the young to mature, and the greater availability of food.

Getting Around

Silent flight. An extra fuzzy covering over the flight feathers quiets the rush of the air over their short, wide and powerful wings, tucks its head in and holds its wings straight out, alternating strong wing beats with glides. On the ground, it walks in alternating steps.

Where to Look

Statewide, but not as common in the northeast. Look for it near open areas, perched on poles, fence posts, trees and rock outcrops scanning for food.
· A *Super Adaptor*

Year-round	Summer
Migration	Winter

Wild Turkey

Meleagris gallopavo

Length: 3–3½ feet
Wingspan: 4–5½ feet

non-displaying male

female

Hens wear dull brown camouflage

Broad, rounded wings and tail. Toms (males) have a tail that spreads into a large fan.

Bare red and blue head and neck with wattle (bumpy skin under the chin that puffs out)

Male: Long, black beard; modified feather tufts 9 inches or more

Body or contour feathers are broad and squared on the ends

Long legs, with spur on back—both males and females have spurs, but only the young males grow into pointed and curved spurs up to 2 inches long

"Gobble, gobble!" or, "This is my territory! Males stay away. Females come on over!"

Trading for Turkeys

Habitat loss. Hunting without limits. Wild Turkeys lost their place in the deciduous woods of the upper Midwest from the 1800s to early 1900s. In 1970, dealmakers at the Minnesota DNR decided to bring Wild Turkeys here as a nesting species. Minnesota had extra Walleyes, Ruffed Grouse, Hungarian Partridges and Greater Prairie-Chickens. So they traded with Missouri, one of the few states where Wild Turkeys still roamed. This resulted in more little jakes and jennies in the forests of southeastern Minnesota. By 1978, the state opened a hunting season for Wild Turkeys. About 60,000 hens and gobblers now roam Minnesota. Happy Thanksgiving!

Habitat Café

Today's Special

pebbles that go into the gizzard to grind food

Yumm . . . bring an order of buds, ferns, bugs, seeds, fruit, grass, nuts (acorns), field grains and more. Wild Turkeys are omnivorous.

SPRING, SUMMER, FALL MENU:
Fruit, berries, insects and plants

FALL MENU:
Acorns and hickory nuts

WINTER MENU:
Corn and other grains from fields

Life Cycle

NEST The female builds the nest in dead leaves on the ground, often hidden under a log, in a bush or at the base of a tree. She lines the nest depression with dry leaves. Mom camouflages the nest and eggs with more leaves when she takes a recess from incubation.

EGGS About 2½ inches long. The female incubates the clutch of 8–15 eggs for 27–28 days. Dad is busy grouping up with his harem of several females.

MOM! DAD! Precocial and downy. The newly hatched chicks leave the nest within one day of hatching. Mom leads them to food where they feed on protein-rich insects, seeds and berries. For warmth and protection from predators, the chicks nestle under Mom's wing next to her body. The young birds have their wing feathers and can fly at two weeks of age. They fly up to a nearby tree branch where they spend the night roosting.

JUVENILE The brood stays together until winter when several hens and their broods join together in a large flock. Toms and jakes form their own flocks.

Gross Factor

How do you know if you are on the trail of a tom or hen? Scat. Poop. Yes, male and female turkeys leave different scat. Males, or toms, leave a J-shaped scat over ⅜-inch in diameter. Females, or hens, leave a curly clump less than ⅜ inch in diameter. Look also for the tracks of wild turkeys that are typically 4–5 inches long and 4¼–5¼ inches wide. Turkeys use their feet to uncover insects, acorns and field corn. Look for scratch marks in the snow, too.

When

Wild Turkeys are diurnal, active during the day, feeding in the early morning and afternoon, and resting in trees at night.

Migration

Permanent resident. Wild Turkeys stay in Minnesota all year.

Nesting

Wild Turkeys begin nesting in April–May in Minnesota.

Getting Around

Fly straight up then away, hard and fast through the treetops at speeds of up to 55 mph over short distances. Can run 18 mph for short distances.

Where to Look

Forested areas near open farm fields, wooded river bottoms, and brushy grasslands. Across the southern half of Minnesota as far north as Kanabec County in the east and up to Mahnomen County in the northwest.
· Beaver Creek Valley State Pk
· Great River Bluffs State Pk
· Whitewater Wildlife Mgmt Area
· Cannon River Wilderness between Faribault and Northfield
· Forestville State Pk
· Eagle Bluffs Enviormental Learning Ctr
· Garvin Park
· Camden State Pk

Year-round Migration	Summer Winter

Deciduous Forest Habitat

Prairie and Open Grasslands

Think like a Western Meadowlark. It needs water, insects for food, tall plants for perches, and a lot of open space without trees. The prairies and open grasslands of southern and western Minnesota are just what a meadowlark needs.

Key to the Future

A prairie is land covered with native grasses and flowering plants with few to no trees at all. Why? Over ten thousand years ago, the Wisconsin Glacier (a mile thick slab of ice) covered Minnesota. As it grew southward it scraped the land, taking with it rocks and soil. When the glacier thawed, the melt-water formed potholes (wetlands) and lakes. The glacier also left behind the rocks and dirt left inside of it, called glacial till. This laid the base for plants to grow.

Fragmented prairie

As the plants died back each year and decayed, new soil formed. This cycle went on for thousands of years, creating soil up to two feet deep—rich, black prairie soil full of nutrients and home to an incredible variety of wild plants and animals.

What is Minnesota's most endangered major habitat? Prairie. At one time, 18 million acres of prairie covered what is now western Minnesota. Today just one percent (about 150,000 acres) of our native prairies remain. We need prairies. Wildlife needs prairies. Native prairie plants and animals hold possible cures to diseases and secrets to make our world a better place to live. Efforts to save what is left and to restore native prairies offer keys to your future. Go to a prairie. Find the treasures and solve the mysteries that are waiting for you.

Mind-boggling Plants

Prairie plants are adapted to survive some pretty harsh conditions. Summer is hot and windy with occasional droughts (long periods without water). Winter brings cold, snow and more wind.

Many prairie plants send their roots deep to reach water and to anchor themselves against the strong winds of the prairie. The Compass Plant grows a taproot ten feet into the rich soil. Other plants send out many fine roots just a few inches under the soil.

Canada anemone

It's cold? Put on a fur coat! This is exactly what some prairie plants do; they grow extra hairs that act like fur to protect them from the drying winds and extreme temperatures.

Dry prairie areas have shorter plants and wet areas host taller plants. In fact, a hundred or more years ago a man could be seen bumping across the prairie riding an invisible horse. The horse was hidden by tall, six- to seven-foot grass!

Pasque Flowers send up their blooms early on short stalks. Plants that bloom later in the summer send up tall stalks to reach the sunlight. The Canada Anemone even grows sections like floors to a high-rise building, adding a "floor" as the prairie grows taller over the summer. On a native prairie there can be more than 25 different kinds of plants in just one square foot! Each species of plant plays host to prairie wildlife.

Incredible Critters

Plants aren't the only things adapted to survive on the prairie. Insects, amphibians, reptiles, mammals and birds have some tricks of their own.

The American Goldfinch, for example, doesn't migrate south with other birds in autumn. It puts on a coat of warmer feathers and stays for the winter, feeding in large flocks with other goldfinches. The flocks' leap-frogging flights over fields help protect the birds from predators. Another open grassland species, the Killdeer, does fly south in fall. But while it's here, it lures predators away from its nest, eggs and young with a dramatic, broken-wing drama that biologists call "injury-feigning display."

American Goldfinch in winter plumage

Scientific and Natural Areas are a great place to spy on birds such as these, and view native prairies as they once were; but you can also find many prairie birds in open grasslands and field edges almost across most of our state. What fascinating prairie birds can you spy on Minnesota's prairie and grasslands? Turn the pages. Prairie wildlife is waiting for you!

Check Off the Prairie Birds You See!

When you spot prairie birds, use these pages to check them off. The locations of these illustrations indicate where you might see them.

III

American Goldfinch

Carduelis tristis

Length: 5 inches
Wingspan: 9 inches

male winter

female

Females are olive-green with pale yellow chest and throat. No black cap.

Black cap

The male is bright yellow in summer, olive-green in winter

Juveniles look like an adult female

White rump

Black tail is notched

"Po-ta-to-chip!" means "This is my space!"

(Sounds like a squeeze-toy.)

Leap Froggin' Goldfinch

Cold, wind, ice and snow send many birds packing their feathers and heading south for the winter. They are looking for warmth and food. American Goldfinches stay. They have adapted to Minnesota's chilly winters, and the change from the large food supply of summer to a limited winter store of seeds. In fact, they can make winter feeding look like a group game! Taking turns in leap frog fashion over mass seed sources is an efficient (energy saving and safe) way for goldfinches to feed in large winter flocks. This rolling motion over a field helps to protect the flock from predators. Your turn . . . .

Habitat Café

Yumm ... bring an order of thistle seed and spring tree buds salted with aphids. Fill your backyard bird feeder with Nyjer thistle seed. Birds can become dependent on seed supplies. Once you start filling the feeder, keep it all year. American Goldfinches are herbivores. Cone-shaped bill used to break open seeds.

SPRING, SUMMER, FALL, WINTER MENU:
Mostly seeds, a few insects

Life Cycle

NEST The female builds the cup-shaped nest, 2–20 feet above the ground in the fork of a thistle, shrub or a deciduous tree. With spider silk, she weaves a nest base to the support branches. Next, rootlets are woven in. Soft thistle down is added last. The nest is so compact (tight), it can hold water like a cup!

EGGS About ½ inch long. The female incubates the 4–6 eggs for 12–14 days. The male feeds her regurgitated (spit-up) food from his crop. Gross, but it works!

MOM! DAD! Altricial. Both Mom and Dad feed the young. At first, Dad feeds Mom, and then she feeds the chicks. This is the routine for the first four days.

NESTLING Feathers replace the chick's first down when they are 12 days old, about the time they are ready to leave the nest.

FLEDGLING Young goldfinches continue to be cared for by the male for three more weeks. They can then forage for seeds on their own.

JUVENILE Juveniles group with other goldfinches and move to areas with plenty of food. In one year, they can nest on their own.

Did You Know?

Most parent birds feed their young a diet of high-protein insects. American Goldfinches feed their young seeds. When Brown-headed Cowbirds lay their eggs in the nest of a goldfinch, the cowbird chicks die (see the Baltimore Oriole on page 82 about cowbird habits). The seed diet does not have enough protein for cowbird chicks to live. The goldfinch chicks then have the full attention of their parents.

When

The American Goldfinch is diurnal. It feeds during the day and rests at night.

Migration

Permanent resident. The American Goldfinch may move to central and southern regions of the U.S. during harsh winters. Many stay in Minnesota during the winter as year-round back-yard visitors.

Nesting

Mid July–mid August. When thistle and milkweed down is mature and fluffy, it is time for nesting in Minnesota.

Getting Around

Stretching his wings in slow rhythm, the male flies in spiral circles over the nesting area. He sings his most impressive, 'po-ta-to-chip.' Two or three males join, each circling in crisscross paths like fluttering bright-yellow butterflies. Biologists call this behavior a Butterfly Flight Pattern.

Where to Look

Open grassland, rural fields and native prairies through most of Minnesota.
· Backyard thistle seed feeders
· Pine to Prairie Birding Trail
· Great River Birding Trail

| Year-round | Summer |
| Migration | Winter |

Grasshopper Sparrow

Ammodramus savannarum

Length: 5–5½ inches
Wingspan: 7–7½ inches

Dark crown with a white head stripe

Brown, rust, and white markings blend in with dried field grasses

Males and females look the same

Half the size of a robin, it is one of Minnesota's smallest sparrows. Its voice is as quiet as a grasshopper's chirp.

Tail is short and stubby, feathers are narrow and pointed

"Tip-tup-a-zeee!"
The male sings this song,
"This is my space.
How about a date?"

Flight: Bernoulli's Principle

How does a bird overcome gravity? How does it fly against "drag" (resistance of the air flowing over the bird's body in flight)? Wing shape and physics. If you haven't studied flight in science yet, here is a head's up on Bernoulli's Principle.

"The shape of a bird's wing is the cause of lift. When the air going past the bird splits, the air going over the top, curved part of the wing goes faster than the slower air past the flatter, bottom of the wing. The top and the bottom air then meet at the same time. In Bernoulli's Principle, the slower the air, the more force it has. The slower air going past the bottom of the wing has more force and causes the bird to go up (lift)."

Elizabeth, 7th grade

Habitat Café

Yumm . . . bring an order of ants, beetles, caterpillars and crickets. Grasshopper Sparrows are omnivorous. They eat both plant and animal matter. Their deep bill is used to pick up insects and seeds from the ground.

SPRING, SUMMER, FALL MENU:
Mainly insects, lots of seeds

WINTER MENU:
Less insects and more seeds than during spring, summer and fall

Life Cycle

NEST The female builds the tiny bowl-shaped nest on the ground with a rounded roof. She weaves stems of loose grass into the overhanging plants for the roof. A side entrance is made for quickly running in and out.

EGGS About ½ inch long. The female incubates the 3–6 eggs for 11–12 days.

MOM! DAD! Altricial. Both Mom and Dad help feed the young and remove the fecal sacs (chick diapers). The parents do not fly straight into the nest. That might lead predators to the hidden eggs or chicks. Instead, they land some distance away and walk to the nest. If a predator does come close to the nest, Mom leads it away with a broken wing act. Tricky birds!

NESTLING The chicks are born blind, naked and totally dependent on their parents. By six days of age, their feathers begin to grow in.

FLEDGLING The young run out of the nest when they are eight days old. They are quick chicks!

JUVENILE Juveniles will be ready to date, mate and raise their own young at one year of age.

Gross Factor

Grasshopper Sparrows catch a grasshopper by the thorax (the middle of the three insect body parts) and pinch it. This paralyzes the grasshopper. Time to shake and eat. Before feeding a grasshopper to their young, the adult shakes the grasshopper until the tough and hard-to-digest legs fall off. Gross and interesting!

When

Grasshopper Sparrows are diurnal. They feed during the day and rest at night.

Migration

Spring Arrival: Mid April–May
Fall Departure: Late Aug.–Sept. Migrate at night in small groups to southern U.S. Night migration allows protection from predators, the need for less water, relief from the heat, and stable air currents.

Nesting

Grasshopper Sparrows nest in late May–late June in Minnesota.

Getting Around

Look to the ground. They spend much of the time walking and running in the grass after prey. Males perch on weed stalks to sing their quiet song. Flight is short and quick. They use fast wing beats to make a straight beeline to their destination.

Where to Look

· Large rather than small, fragmented (broken up) open grasslands, fields and prairies.
· Felton Prairie
· McCarthy Wildlife Mgmt Area
· Rothsay Wildlife Mgmt Area
· Lac Qui Parle
· Conservation Reserve Program fields

Year-round	Summer
Migration	Winter

Prairie and Open Grasslands Habitat

Dickcissel

Spiza americana

Length: 6–7 inches
Wingspan: 9–9½ inches

Yellow line over the eye and on the side of the throat

The female is not as brightly colored as the male and does not have a black bib. The young look like the female but are striped below.

The male has a white chin and black bib with yellow below

Rusty patch at bend of wing

Short tail hangs straight down

"See-see-dick, dick, ciss-ciss-cissel!" Males sing this song during nesting season.

Hide and Seek

Where are the Dickcissels? Playing a game of Hide-and-Seek across the grasslands and prairies of Minnesota. Dickcissels change their location and numbers from year to year. They may be in large numbers on a prairie one year, and the next year in much smaller numbers on a different Minnesota grassland. Why? They stay where there is just the right amount of precipitation (rain or snow). A clue to their changing numbers may also be in their Central and South American wintering habitat. These migratory birds live in one part of the world during breeding and nesting season and another part of the world the rest of the year. They depend on teamwork around the world for the care of their habitats.

Today's Special
crickets

Habitat Café

Yumm . . . bring an order of grasshoppers, ants, beetles, bugs, spiders and weed seeds. Adult Dickcissels are omnivorous. With the cold of winter and the loss of their insect food supply, they migrate to Central and South America.

SPRING, SUMMER, FALL MENU:
🐜 Mostly insects, some seeds

WINTER MENU:
🌱 Mostly seeds, some insects

Life Cycle

NEST The female builds the bulky nest cup near the ground, hidden in thick weeds or on a small bush. She weaves weeds, grass stems and leaves to make the base. The nest is then lined with fine grasses, rootlets and the hair and fur of animals.

EGGS About ⅝ inch long. Female incubates the 3–6 eggs for 11–12 days. After the eggs hatch, she drops the shells away from the nest. Recycled egg shells provide calcium for small mammals like voles, shrews, mice and ground squirrels.

MOM! DAD! Altricial. Mom feeds the young and keeps the nest clean by removing the fecal sacs (chick diapers). She may take 20 trips for grasshoppers in one hour to feed her hungry brood!

NESTLING The white downy chicks stay in the nest for 8–10 days.

FLEDGLING Mom feeds the fledglings for the first two weeks they are out of the nest.

JUVENILE In late August and early September, juveniles join with adults in migrating flocks. Blackbirds and Bobolinks may also join the flock. In the spring, they are mature enough to date, mate and nest.

Birding Tip

When is the best time to mow or hay a field when considering nesting birds? Watch the male for clues. While the female is incubating eggs, the male perches on a post or fence to defend the territory. When the young hatch, he is out of sight, hunting and delivering food to the chicks. Small birds need another 2–3 weeks to fly. Mowing after nesting gives young birds a better chance of survival.

When

Dickcissels are diurnal. They feed during the day and rest at night.

Migration

Spring Arrival: Mid to late May
Fall Departure: August–Sept.
Long-distance migrant. Most winter in the Ilanos region (seasonally flooded grasslands) of Central Venezuela. Some migrate to Mexico and Panama.

Nesting

Nest in Minnesota during May–June. Prefer medium-dense and medium-high grasses for nesting area.

Getting Around

Dickcissels walk or hop on the ground. In the air, their flight is quick and direct. On their Central and South American wintering grounds, flocks of up to one million flying Dickcissels can look like a spiraling funnel cloud overhead.

Where to Look

Open grasslands, rural fields and native prairies.
· Blue Mounds State Pk
· Dodge Nature Ctr
· Walnut Lake Wildlife Mgmt Area
· Sherburne Nat'l Wildlife Refuge
· Carlos Avery Wildlife Mgmt Area

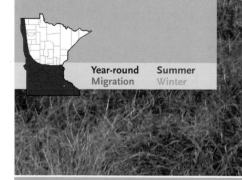

Year-round Migration	Summer Winter

Bobolink

Dolichonyx oryzivorus

Length: 6–8 inches
Wingspan: 11–12 inches

female

Female is buff color with streaks down her back, wings and sides

The male wears his tuxedo backward, a black belly, wings and head set off by white down his back; he is also nicknamed the "skunk bird"

Juveniles look like females without streaks on the side and more yellow underneath

Stiff, pointed tail feathers

"Bob-o-link, bob-o-link, sspink, spank, sspink."
Males, "This is my space. Gals, come over."

Drawing the Line

Male Bobolinks decide where their space (territory) begins and the neighboring male's space ends by doing a boogie called the "Parallel Walk." First they show off their most colorful marking, the yellow patch on the back of the neck. They turn their head down and to the side. Next, the two neighbors hop side by side along an invisible line. This boogie-woogie can go on for hours. "Hey, you're on my side of the line!" Reminds me of the invisible line I had with my sister down the middle of the back seat in the family car.

Habitat Café

Today's Special
caterpillars

Yumm . . . bring an order of spiders, beetles, grasshoppers and crickets. As they migrate, Bobolinks eat large amounts of grain in the "milk" stage. This makes body fat for the long flight south.

SPRING, SUMMER, FALL MENU:
Mainly insects, lots of seeds and grains

WINTER MENU:
Almost all seeds and grains, some insects

Life Cycle

NEST The female builds the nest in an open field. She picks up grasses and builds them around a low area on the ground. Next, she lines the nest with soft, fine grasses.

EGGS About ⅝ inch long. The female incubates the 5–6 eggs for 12–13 days.

MOM! DAD! Altricial. Mom does most of the parenting. Dad has up to four families hatching and hungry at the same time.

NESTLING The newly hatched chicks are naked. They grow feathers by the time they are 10 days old and leave the nest.

FLEDGLING Feathers the same color as the ground help hide the fledglings in a field or prairie. They can fly on their own at 15 days of age. They beg for food from their parents until they are 3–4 weeks old.

JUVENILE Juveniles join in a flock with their family group and get ready for fall migration. When they return in the spring, they are mature enough to date (courtship), mate and raise their own young.

Did You Know?

Eggs are laid one each day over 5–6 days, but all hatch within a day or two of each other. Biologists designed experiments to find out how the eggs might be different depending on what day in the line-up they were laid. Eggs laid last had more of a body chemical called testosterone than the eggs laid first. Higher levels of testosterone cause faster growth and more aggressiveness, helping the chicks from the last eggs catch up!

When

Bobolinks are diurnal. They migrate by night in large flocks and rest by day.

Migration

Spring Arrival: mid-May
Fall Departure: late Aug.–Sept.
Long-distance migrant. The Bobolink makes one of the longest migrations of any North American songbird, winging deep into South America, where it spends the winter in "pampas" grass of Brazil and Argentina—it's an 11,000-mile round trip!

Nesting

Bobolinks nest in Minnesota during late May and June.

Getting Around

Boblinks walk slowly while pecking seeds and insects from the ground. Flight during nesting season is fast and low, to keep out of the sight of hungry predators. Long hind toenails allow Bobolinks to perch on plant stems.

Where to Look

Open grassland and rural fields. Prefer native prairies but have adapted to hay fields of at least 1–5 acres in size.
· Felton Prairie
· Sand Prairie Wildlife Mgmt Area
· Schaefer Prairie

Year-round Migration	Summer Winter

Horned Lark

Eremophila alpestris

Length: 7 inches
Wingspan: 12 inches

horns

Black patch on side of head and a black band across forehead

The "horns" are tufts of black feathers

White or yellow throat

Juveniles do not have the black head and throat markings of the adult. "Horns" are formed by two years of age.

Females look like males with a duller color

Black patch on breast

Black tail with white on the sides

"Su-weet!" This sweet song is sung from a perch like a fencepost or shrub.

Aerobatic Antics

Beginning as early as February in Minnesota, the male Horned Lark begins his airborne, "impress the ladies" show. Singing while he flies in a sky-bound spiral, he climbs higher and higher until he is lost in the clouds. Closing his wings, he plunges headfirst toward the prairie. Then, nearly scraping the ground, he opens his wings, turns and climbs skyward to perform his daring display all over again. He hopes the female Horned Larks are wowed, awed and rendered totally chirpless.

Today's Special
seeds

Habitat Café

Yumm . . . bring an order of small weed seeds, hold the onions, please. Adult Horned Larks eat mostly seeds with a few insects, and are omnivores. They feed protein-rich insects to their chicks for fast growth.

SPRING, SUMMER, FALL MENU:
Mostly seeds, some insects

WINTER MENU:
More seeds and fewer insects than during spring, summer and fall

Life Cycle

NEST The female builds the nest beginning with a shallow dip in the ground, near or under grass. She makes a nest cup with stems and leaves, lining it with fine grasses.

EGGS About ⅝ inch long. The female incubates the 3–5 pale, grayish white eggs for 11 days.

MOM! DAD! Altricial. Both Mom and Dad help feed the young. On average, a very young chick can expect food once every 5–6 minutes. Their eyes open when they are 4 days old.

NESTLING The chicks hatch with a downy covering, ready for the chilly, early spring temperatures.

FLEDGLING Young Horned Larks leave the nest at 10 days old, when they have their primary feathers. They can walk and fly like an adult when they are 27 days old.

JUVENILE Juvenile larks gather in small groups throughout the summer, go through their first molt (old feathers fall out and new feathers grow in) and prepare to migrate by October.

Unsolved Mystery

Female Horned Larks have been seen placing small pebbles on one side of the nest rim. Are they building a nest patio? Are the pebbles a way to hold down the grasses while she works on the nest? Use your scientific detective skills to find the answer to this unsolved mystery!

When

Horned Larks are diurnal. They feed during the day and rest at night.

Migration

Spring Arrival: Jan.–March
Fall Departure: October
The Horned Lark is a short-distance migrant that moves to central, southern and southeastern regions of the U.S. Some larks return to Minnesota as early as January.

Nesting

The Horned Lark likes to get a jump on the nesting season. It nests in southern Minnesota in early spring, even while there is snow cover; 1–3 broods per year are possible.

Getting Around

Horned Larks forage (look for food) on the ground in crop fields, gravel roadsides and in fields and prairies of short grasses. In flight, their wings beat 3–4 times; then are folded against the body for the time of 1–2 beats.

Where to Look

· Open grassland and rural fields
· Felton Prairie
· Red Rock Prairie
· Blue Mounds State Pk

Year-round   Summer
Migration   Winter

American Kestrel

Falco sparverius

Length: 7–8 inches
Wingspan: 20–24 inches

female

Black-and-white
face pattern

Markings on the back of
the head look like a pair of
false eyes or "ocelli"

Hooked,
sharp beak

Females have red-brown
wings and seven to nine
dark bands across the tail.
Brown-streaked breast.
Female larger than male.

Narrow body,
long tail

Juveniles look like
adults with dull colors

"Killy, killy, killy"
means
"Stay away!"

Highway Neighbors

Look closely at the back of highway signs on your road trips. The Minnesota DNR Nongame Wildlife Program has placed kestrel nest boxes along U.S. Highway 10 in central Minnesota from Motley to St. Cloud. In southern Minnesota, look along I-90 and State Highway 60 from Madelia to St. James. Be involved. Build a nest box for kestrels. Ask your local conservation officer for the best place to hang a nest box. Include a hinged lid to carefully check the inside of the box during nesting season and keep a record of the number of eggs, young and adults. Make an older tree in your yard or woodlot a wildlife tree and watch for these handy neighbors as they eat unwelcome insects and rodents!

Today's Special

ground squirrels

Habitat Café

Yumm . . . bring an order of mice, snakes, lizards, caterpillars, beetles, dragonflies, crickets and a few small birds and animals. American Kestrels are carnivorous. Kestrel parents plan for the kids' extra snacks and poor weather conditions by caching uneaten prey in grass clumps, tree roots, holes and limbs or a fence post.

SPRING, SUMMER, FALL MENU:
Mostly insects, some birds and animals

WINTER MENU:
All small animals

Life Cycle

NEST Kestrels prefer to nest in a woodpecker hole or natural tree cavity at the edge of a wooded area. With the loss of nesting habitat, they have adapted to using nest boxes near their food prey. They do not bring in nesting materials, but may add feathers. A few wood chips may be placed in the bottom of a nest box.

EGGS About 1⅛ inches long. The female incubates the 4–5 eggs for 30 days. The male takes over when the female leaves for a short time each day. Both have a "brood patch," an area on the belly without feathers. Putting a bare belly to eggs keeps them warm.

MOM! DAD! Altricial. Both Mom and Dad help feed the young.

NESTLING The brown-gray chicks stay in the nest for 30 days. Young kestrels shoot their feces (body wastes) onto the upper walls of the nest cavity. The bottom of the nest stays fairly clean.

FLEDGLING Parents feed the young for the first 14 days after they leave the nest.

JUVENILE The first year is the hardest for birds to survive. In a research study, only 4 out of 10 kestrels reached their first birthday.

Gross Factor

Kestrel table manners: Large insects are eaten head and guts first (the most nutritious parts). When the dining menu includes small birds, the head is ripped off and devoured, followed by the breast and upper belly. Snacking on the legs and feet, optional. What happens to the leftovers? Dermestid beetles clean the mess up right away. Yum.

When

American Kestrels are diurnal. They feed during the day and rest at night.

Migration

Spring Arrival: mid March
Fall Departure: October
Some kestrels stay in Minnesota until snow covers the ground and prey is hard to find. Some migrate as far south as Mexico and Panama.

Nesting

American Kestrels nest in Minnesota during late April and June.

Getting Around

Kestrels hover in one place by facing into the wind with their wings spread. Their boomerang-shaped wings have a notch in the outer three primary feathers to aid in hovering. The tail is used as a rudder to steady the bird while it searches for prey on the ground. Flight pattern: Deep-rowing wing beats. Kestrels perch on utility lines and poles and look for prey.

Where to Look

Most of Minnesota along highways, railroad tracks, rural roadsides, pastures and open fields.
· Pine to Prairie Birding Trail

Year-round	Summer
Migration	Winter

Eastern Kingbird

Tyrannus tyrannus

Length: 8 inches
Wingspan: 15 inches

white tail band

Black head with hidden red "king's" crown. When excited, the male raises his head feathers to show off his crown.

White chin

Gray on top with a white belly and underside

Males, females and juveniles look very much alike

Black tail with white band

"Chatter-zeer" could be "Hi. I'm back." Or a male telling others that he's patrolling his territory.

Tyrant of the Air

Tyrants are bullies. *Tyrannosaurus rex* dinosaurs are known for bullying other dinosaurs, way back in earth history. *Tyrannus tyrannus*, the Eastern Kingbird, is known today for bullying bigger birds to claim its territory and protect its young. If a hawk, crow or owl flies even 100 feet above an Eastern Kingbird nest, watch out. The kingbird will mount a full aerial attack that includes chasing and crashing into the bigger bird from above while screeching, *Zeeeer!* The predator is . . . out of there.

Today's Special
fresh wasps

Habitat Café

Yumm . . . bring an order of dragonflies, drone bumblebees, beetles and grasshoppers. Eastern Kingbirds are omnivorous. They feed on insects in Minnesota and fruits in their South American wintering grounds.

SPRING, SUMMER, FALL MENU:
Almost entirely insects, some berries

WINTER MENU:
Mostly fruit, a few insects

Life Cycle

NEST The female builds the messy but sturdy nest 10–20 feet above the ground with plant stems and small twigs on a tree limb. She lines the nest with soft cottonwood or cattail down.

EGGS About ¾ inch long. The female incubates the clutch of 3–4 eggs for 14–16 days.

MOM! DAD! Altricial. Both Mom and Dad help feed the young.

NESTLING The chicks hatch naked with orange skin and their eyes closed. After the first day, the colorful skin changes to gray and feathers begin to form.

FLEDGLING The young normally leave the nest when they are able to fly weakly, at about 16–18 days old. The parents kill the prey, mostly flying insects, and remove the stingers from bees and wasps before feeding them to the young. Ouch! What parents will do for their kids!

JUVENILE Juveniles stay in the family group until just before fall migration. They are ready to date, mate and raise their own young when they return to Minnesota in the spring.

Gross Factor

Kingbirds wait on their perch for a flying insect to come near. They snatch it from the air in a short, quick flight called "hawking." Once a large insect is caught, the kingbird takes it to its perch, pounds it on a branch until it doesn't move, then eats it whole. Dragonfly wings can be scratchy going down!

When

Eastern Kingbirds are diurnal. They feed during the day and rest at night.

Migration

Spring Arrival: May
Fall Departure: Late August–early September, Minnesota peak. Long-distance migrant. Migrate during the day in flocks of 10–60 birds to Central and South America, as far as Peru and Argentina.

Nesting

Eastern Kingbirds nest in Minnesota during June.

Getting Around

Perch on plants, fence posts or branches in prairie and rural fields, roadsides, forest edges, marsh or lake edges. Male does a "tumble flight." First, he flies high in a fluttering flight. Next, in short glides and aerobatic tumbles, he falls to the earth, Red Baron style. Good grief!

Where to Look

Grasslands, prairies and fields. Look for Eastern Kingbirds perched on dead branches along a central Minnesota lake, while you're fishing for bass, panfish or a toothy northern pike.
· Rothsay WMA

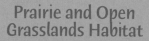

Year-round	Summer
Migration	Winter

Burrowing Owl

Athene cunicularia

Length: 8½–10 inches tall
Wingspan: 21–22 inches

Round head with an oval facial ruff

Bright, lemon yellow eyes

The young will look like their parents at the end of their first year

Brown back with white spots

Brown with white speckles above, white with brown bars underneath

Long, rounded wings

The female and male look the same, but females are darker

Short tail with big feathers that help in flight direction

"Rattle, rattle." Young Burrowing Owls make a rattle call to scare away predators.

Beating the Heat

Hot. Very hot is the best way to describe a Minnesota prairie and open field in the summer. How do Burrowing Owls beat the heat? They droop their long wings over their body like a shield. Underground burrows are cool and moist. This basement-level home gives them protection from heat and water loss (dehydration). They are called Burrowing Owls because they can dig their own burrow in the ground. However, most often they use a burrow made by badgers. They clean out the former owner's leftovers and pile them in a mound outside the burrow. The mound makes a great lookout for danger!

Habitat Café

Yumm . . . bring an order of grasshoppers, beetles, crickets, lizards, mice, ground squirrels, pocket gophers and small birds. Both adults and juveniles will eat their weight in food every 24 hours. Burrowing Owls are carnivorous.

SPRING, SUMMER, FALL, WINTER MENU:
A balanced diet of insects, reptiles, amphibians, mammals and birds

Life Cycle

NEST Burrowing Owls can make their own nests by kicking backward with their feet and digging with their beak, but rarely go to all this trouble. Instead, they depend on badgers to dig burrows and then take them over (once the badger has moved out, of course).

EGGS About 1 inch long. The female incubates the clutch of 7–10 eggs for 28–30 days.

MOM! DAD! Altricial. Burrowing Owl chicks hatch with their eyes closed. Unable to leave the burrow, they depend on their parents for food and care. For the first two weeks, Dad does all the grocery shopping, catching prey. Both parents help feed the young.

NESTLING At two weeks of age, the young venture out of the burrow, standing at the entrance waiting for Dad and Mom to bring lunch.

FLEDGLING They leave the burrow when they are about 44 days old, but hang around the house to go hunting with Mom and Dad. They are about the same size as their parents when they leave the burrow.

JUVENILE When 7–8 weeks of age, the young begin to catch their own food and live in a nearby burrow.

Unsolved Mystery

A horse in a hole? Is that what a Burrowing Owl intends for a predator to smell when they put horse manure (dung) on the outside entrance of their burrow? Experiments have not yet proven this to be true. What other reason might there be for this stinky welcome mat? Go ahead, stick your nose into this unsolved mystery.

When
Burrowing Owls are diurnal, nocturnal and crepuscular, depending on the time of year. This means that they may be out and about just about any time, night or day.

Migration
Spring Arrival: April–May
Fall Departure: Sept.–Oct.

Nesting
Average date of egg laying in Minnesota is mid-May.

Getting Around
Burrowing Owls walk, hop and run on the ground after their prey. They also hunt by hovering over tall or dense vegetation, and catching insects in flight. Except during their migration, most flying is limited to short-distance hops from ground to a perch.

Where to Look
Burrowing Owls live in short-grass fields and prairies. In west-central Minnesota, they prefer farm pastures with colonies of Richardson's Ground Squirrels. Burrowing Owls are so rare that they are a Minnesota Endangered Species and have special protection under the law. We can help the Burrowing Owl by respecting its need for wild spaces.

Extremely rare—dots indicate past sightings

Western Meadowlark

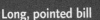

Sturnella neglecta

Length: 9 inches
Wingspan: 14 inches

Dark crown

Long, pointed bill

Meadowlarks have the beautiful song of a lark but they are in the blackbird family

Black V on chest

Bright yellow breast and belly

Males are larger and females are not as brightly colored

Short tail with white margins in flight

Long legs and toes

"Whistle!" means "Danger! Stay low to the ground and freeze!"

Woolly Mammoths and Meadowlarks

What do they have in common? Fossil records show that they both lived in this area over 10,000 years ago. Woolly Mammoths are extinct; there are no more Woolly Mammoths living on earth. Meadowlarks are still here, but there are fewer and fewer with the loss of their habitat. Male meadowlarks use 5–7 acres of grassland for their breeding territory (space). What can you do? In rural Minnesota, set aside a large grassy area free of chemicals and predators. Wait to mow, hay, or graze the area until after nesting season. Include a tall post for a meadowlark to stretch its bill to the sky and sing. Set up your spotting scope and watch for a new black-bibbed neighbor!

Today's Special
crickets

Habitat Café

Yumm . . . bring an order of beetles, weevils, cutworms and grasshoppers. Meadowlarks are omnivorous, eating both plant and animal matter. They probe for food by "gaping" (putting their closed, pointed bill in the ground or under a rock and spreading it wide).

SPRING, SUMMER MENU:
Mainly insects, some seeds

WINTER MENU:
Mostly fruit and seeds, a few insects

Life Cycle

NEST The female builds a dome-like nest in a grassy field. A deep spot in the ground is filled with large grasses and lined with fine, soft grasses. The dome (about 7 inches high) is built over the top by weaving together plants growing around the nest. A 3–4 inch opening is left on one side of the nest with a path through the grass for coming and going.

EGGS About ¾ inch long. The female incubates the 3–5 pale eggs for 13–14 days. If the nest is disturbed, the female will leave and not go back to incubate the eggs. Respect the need for safe nesting.

MOM! DAD! Altricial. Mom does most of the feeding. Dad does not go to the nest. He catches insects and "beaks" them over to Mom.

NESTLING Nestlings need to eat more than half of their body weight in food each day. That calls for a lot of beetles, grasshoppers...

FLEDGLING With long, quick legs and the ability to hide in plants, the young leave the nest at 10–12 days old. Their parents feed them for two more weeks, until they can fly.

JUVENILE They look like their parents but with spots instead of a black bib on their chest. In one year, they are mature enough to nest.

Did You Know?

Each meadowlark male has his own combination of flute-like notes with six or more song compositions. Meadowlarks learn songs from their parents when they are young. If they do not hear their parents' song, they will learn a song from another bird. A Western Meadowlark has even taken on the song of a Northern Cardinal!

When

Meadowlarks are diurnal. They feed during the day and rest at night.

Migration

Spring Arrival: March–April. Fall Departure: October–Nov. Short to Long-distance migrant. Spends winter in areas with temperatures +10F. Southern Iowa to Mexico. In spring, males arrive two weeks before females to set up territories.

Nesting

Nest in Minnesota beginning April–May. Raise 1–2 broods per nesting season.

Getting Around

Meadowlarks walk and run on the ground. When a female meadowlark nears her nest, she walks closer to the ground to hide from predators. Their flight is a series of a glide followed by quick wing beats. They can fly 20–40 miles per hour.

Where to Look

Open grasslands and rural fields across most of Minnesota. (Eastern Meadowlarks live in the eastern half of the state.)
· Rothsay Wildlife Mgmt Area
· Afton State Pk
· Western Prairie Scientific and Natural Area
· U of MN, St. Paul campus agriculture fields

Year-round	Summer
Migration	Winter

Prairie and Open Grasslands Habitat

Killdeer

Charadrius vociferus

Length: 9–11 inches
Wingspan: 24 inches

nesting

injury-feigning display

The downy young and juveniles have only one black band across their breast

Olive-brown

Both the male and the female have two black bands across their breast

Rusty orange rump patch is seen when tail is spread

White underside

Long legs for wading in the shallow water and running fast

"Kill—deer, kill—deer!" or, "Sound the alarm! Danger near!"

Best Drama Award

The Killdeer spread out and crushed on the ground in front of you looks like a dying bird uttering its last painful *dee*. Bringing itself from sure death, the Killdeer limps along with a broken wing. Watch it long enough and the wings may go from being broken to healed, broken to healed. Poor bird? Smart, tricky bird, that has just lured a predator away from its eggs or young. This behavior is called "injury-feigning display." Your part in this drama is that of a responsible neighbor. Leave the nesting area to watch from afar with your spotting scope or binoculars. Your reward will be more Killdeer to watch in the future. Take a bow.

Today's Special
crayfish

Habitat Café

Yumm . . . bring an order grasshoppers, beetles, earthworms, ticks, and mosquito larvae with a side of Green Treefrog. Killdeer are omnivorous.

SPRING, SUMMER, FALL MENU:
Mostly insects, crustaceans and amphibians, some seeds

WINTER MENU:
Entirely insects and crustaceans

Life Cycle

NEST The nest is a simple, low scrape in the ground. It is lined with material found nearby, such as pebbles, gravel or woodchips, which help keep the eggs from rolling away with the wind or rain.

EGGS About 1½ inches long. Both the male and female incubate the 4 camouflaged eggs for 24–25 days.

MOM! DAD! Precocial. Parent Killdeer do not feed the chicks. As soon as the chicks have hatched and their down is dry, the parents lead them to feeding areas. Parents brood the young for the first few days and guard them for the first ten days. Chicks can swim across small streams.

FLEDGLING If a predator comes near, chicks lay low and freeze. Some will raise their leg above the grass to look like a stem or stick. This is a bird that uses acting for predator control. Killdeer stay with their parents and siblings until they can fly at 20–30 days old.

JUVENILE Killdeer can nest and mate when they are one year of age.

Did You Know?

Nesting on a rooftop can be dangerous. Killdeer in this situation can be creative when it is time to lead their newly hatched chicks to food. One pair of Killdeer parents called to their chicks from the ground near the base of a rain gutter. The chicks heard the parents call to come down from the roof and they used the rainspout as a slide. Wheee . . . .

When

Killdeer are diurnal. They feed during the day and rest at night. Migrate by day and night.

Migration

Spring Arrival: March–April
Fall Departure: Late Sept.–Oct. Long-distance migrant. Killdeer migrate south in flocks of up to 30 birds to Central and South America. They are one of the first spring arrivals to Minnesota.

Nesting

Killdeer nest in Minnesota from mid-April through mid-May.

Getting Around

Killdeer have a standard ground move: run a short ways, stop, bob their head and run again. They keep their body straight while their long legs are a blur of motion. In flight, they are strong and fast at speeds of 28–35 miles per hour. Adult Killdeer can swim in fast-flowing water.

Where to Look

Originally a shorebird found on mud flats and sandbars, the Killdeer has adapted to open habitats: fields, grazed pastures, golf courses, gravel parking lots, flat gravel rooftops, soccer fields, airports and playgrounds.
· Most of Minnesota
· A *Super Adaptor*

Year-round	Summer
Migration	Winter

Greater Prairie-Chicken

Tympanuchus cupido

Length: 17–18 inches
Wingspan: 28 inches

female

Females are mostly brown with light barring

Males blow up their orange neck sacs and raise their orange "eyebrows" and feathers during their mating dance

The pinnae feathers look like horns

Males have a short, rounded, dark tail with no barring

Booming is made by forcing air past their syrinx (vocal cords). It is made louder with their speaker system, esophageal air sacs.

"BOOM, BOOM, BOOM.." or, "This is MY territory!"

"Tympanuchus crowing and, in ecstasy, emitting many other queer sounds."
Dr. Johann Hvoslef, Lanesboro, Minnesota, April 3, 1902

What Dr. Johann Hvoslef wrote in his journal on April 3, 1902, was likely describing male Greater Prairie-Chickens. Their cackling, foot stomping, wing shaking, tail clicking and whooping would have made quite a noise. They can boom at a rate of 10 booms per second, which can be heard over two miles away! A lek, or booming ground, may have 6 to 10 males at one time. This spring and summer band played across the prairies of southern and western Minnesota during the 1800s to early 1900s. Not today. Most of the habitat for leks and nesting is gone. Visit a protected prairie area they still call home to hear the same wild song and dance that Dr. Hvoslef heard.

Habitat Café

Yumm . . . bring an order of plant seeds, beetles, ants and grasshoppers. Greater Prairie-Chickens are omnivorous. They walk along the ground and forage for food.

SPRING, SUMMER, FALL, WINTER MENU:
Mostly seeds, berries and plants, some insects

Life Cycle

NEST The female builds a bowl-shaped nest in the ground with stems and grasses. She lines it with fine grasses and feathers. Pheasant hens will sneak into the nest and lay their own eggs. The Greater Prairie-Chicken hen will often leave the nest with baby pheasants in tow. Her own unhatched chicks are left behind because prairie-chicken eggs take longer to hatch.

EGGS About 1¾ inches long. The hen incubates the 10–14 eggs for 23–26 days. Hens take recesses in the early morning and late evening to feed.

MOM! DAD! Precocial. The chicks have some feathers when they hatch. They soon leave the nest to feed on insects and seeds. The hen broods the young for the first two weeks—the time it takes for their feathers to grow all the way in.

JUVENILE Juveniles have brown, patterned feathers that look like the plants around them. They need the disguise. Predators (foxes, hawks, coyotes) are looking for a meal. Less than half of the young will make it to their second year. The first winter, juveniles flock together or move to a wintering area. They can breed after their first year.

History Hangout

Prairie-chickens spread across Minnesota with the plowing of the prairies and logging in the north until 1900, when they were found in suitable grassy habitat statewide. But intensified agriculture and the regrowth of timber led to their widespread demise. By 1960 they were limited to hard-to-farm areas in west-central Minnesota. Thanks to state, federal and private habitat help, their range is again expanding.

When

Greater Prairie-Chickens are diurnal. They feed during the day and rest at night.

Migration

Nonmigratory.
Most Greater Prairie-Chickens remain in their home area during the winter. Some may move to areas miles away in the fall. To survive the winter, they tunnel under the snow to roost at night.

Nesting

Nest during May and June in western Minnesota's protected areas.

Getting Around

They fly in a pattern of fast wing beats followed by a glide. Once they get to a sail-glide, they can fly 40–50 mph. In attack fights, males lower their pinnae feathers, let the air out of their orange sacs, leap in the air and with full force, attack with their beak, wings and feet. It can be a fight to the death.

Where to Look

Public areas from Thief River Falls to Rothsay and farther south.
· Tympanuchus Wildlife Mgmt Area
· Rothsay Wildlife Mgmt Area
· Pembina Trail Preserve Scientific and Natural Area
· Felton Prairie

Year-round	Summer
Migration	Winter

Northern Harrier

Circus cyaneus

Length: 16–24 inches
Wingspan: 3½–4 feet

Males are silver gray above and lighter below

White rump patch

wheeling

female

The females are brown above and cream and brown streaked below, with a banded tail

Black wingtips

Juveniles look similar to females, but are darker brown above and russet below

Long, square tail

♪ "Kek, kek, kek" means "Stay away!" ♪

Flying Food Pass

Watch Northern Harriers during the summer. Watch closely. You may see the male perform a flying food pass. When he has a juicy mouse, he signals to the female on the nest below, "purrduk." She flies just under him, turns over and catches the mouse in her talons. A speedy delivery is made to the hungry chicks. Keep watch for Northern Harriers to pick up a mouse nest, shake it, then drop the nest. A litter of young mice and their parents are snatched up for a quick snack. How do they know the nest is full of mice? As they glide over Minnesota's grassy fields and prairies, harriers hear prey before they see it with a facial disk that funnels sound to their enlarged ear openings.

Habitat Café

Yumm . . . bring an order of mice, shrews, frogs, lizards and small perching birds. Northern Harriers are carnivorous. They eat only animal matter. They hunt low over the ground with their slim, lightweight body, long wings and keen sense of hearing.

SPRING, SUMMER, FALL, WINTER MENU:

 Entirely animal matter

Life Cycle

NEST The female builds a pile of grass and weeds on the ground, hollowed in the top with a few sticks or twigs as the base.

EGGS About 1¾ inches long. The female incubates 4–6 eggs for 30 days. The male brings her food and may shade or guard the eggs while she takes a break.

MOM! DAD! Altricial. Dad brings the food to Mom. She feeds the kids by tearing the food into small pieces as they take it from her bill. Unlike their quiet parents, the chicks use noisy screech calls to scare predators.

NESTLING When Junior strays from the nest, Mom carries it back home in her bill by the nape (back of neck). After two weeks of age, the young have paths through the grass to raised feeding and resting areas.

FLEDGLING Heavy as an adult, they can fly at one month of age and their meals come in an aerial pass from their parents. To practice capturing prey, the young pounce on objects on the ground.

JUVENILE Juveniles join with others their age, feeding and preparing for migration. It takes 2–3 years to gain their adult plumage and be mature enough to raise their own young.

Birding Tip

LOOK OUT OVERHEAD! These strong birds of prey will dive at and possibly even sink their talons into anyone that gets close to the nest. It's a good idea not to disturb any bird nest or nesting area during this sensitive time. Adults may abandon the young and you may be in danger. Safety first, for everyone!

When

Northern Harriers are diurnal. They can spend 40 percent of their day in flight, logging up to 100 miles per day!

Migration

Spring Arrival: March
Fall Departure: November
Long-distance migrant. Flying alone, they migrate to Texas, Mexico, Costa Rica and Panama. With good soaring conditions they migrate close to the ground.

Nesting

Nest in Minnesota during early May.

Getting Around

Look for Northern Harriers in an open field flying low (10–13 feet) over the ground scanning the ground and listening for lunch. They fly with a series of flaps and tilting glides, their wings held in a spread-out V. Three to five outer primary wing feathers are notched for aerodynamic soaring.

Where to Look

Wetlands, undisturbed grasslands and native prairies in Minnesota. Watch for harriers especially during migration.
· Glacial Ridge Nat'l Wildlife Refuge
· Agassiz Nat'l Wildlife Refuge
· Wetlands, Pine and Prairie Audubon Sanctuary

Year-round	Summer
Migration	Winter

Red-tailed Hawk

Buteo jamaicensis

Length: 18–25 inches
Wingspan: 4–5 feet

soaring

Dark head and upper side, lighter underside

White underside with brown streaks on belly that may resemble a band

Male and female look the same, but the female is larger, stronger

Tail is "red" on upper side with a narrow, dark band

Only adult hawks have red tails

"Kee-eee-arr!" or, "This is my territory."

Hawk Ridge, Duluth

Explore Hawk Ridge in Duluth, Minnesota, in mid- to late October. It's called Hawk Ridge for a reason. Sixteen species of hawks use the rising thermals and the safety of Lake Superior's shoreline. They migrate south by the thousands along this route. Red-tailed Hawks soar above the ridge (often at eye level) from September to November. The average annual count of Red-tailed Hawks passing over Hawk Ridge is nearly 5,000. They can be seen all over Minnesota and have become more common along highways in the Twin Cities area. Look for them perched on power lines, in trees and on billboards as they scan roadside ditches for a meal of rabbits and rodents. (Drivers, watch the road!)

Today's Special
muskrats

Habitat Café

Yumm . . . bring an order of rabbits, mice, voles, chipmunks, squirrels, snakes, gophers, skinks and pheasants. Red-tailed Hawks are carnivorous. Sharp, hooked beak and talons are used for capturing and tearing apart prey. Taken to a feeding perch, small mammals are swallowed whole and birds are beheaded, plucked and eaten. Bill-licking good.

SPRING, SUMMER, FALL, WINTER MENU:
Mostly mammals, some reptiles, birds and amphibians

Life Cycle

NEST The male and female build the bulky nest in a large tree, 30–90 feet from the ground. They may return to the same nest for several years, adding more sticks and lining it with moss, evergreen twigs and grapevine bark. Nests that are reused for years can be over three feet deep!

EGGS Slightly more than 2¼ inches long. The female and male incubate the 2–3, dull, creamy white eggs for 28–35 days.

MOM! DAD! Altricial. Both Mom and Dad help feed the young. At first the parents tear off pieces of prey for the chicks, but as they grow, the parents leave the food for the young to tear apart on their own. Learning to be independent is a big thing in the bird world.

NESTLING Fluffy down begins to be replaced by new feathers when the chicks are 16 days of age.

FLEDGLING Young Red-tailed Hawks leave the nest and fly when they are 6–7 weeks old.

JUVENILE Immature has a gray-brown tail with dark bands. It takes two years to develop the red tail. Immature Red-tailed Hawks begin to migrate south before the adults in the fall.

Unsolved Mystery

Red-tailed Hawks put a fresh, leafy branch in the nest with the chicks every day. Why? To shade the young? To hide the young from predators? Do the aromatic oils in the leaves help control parasites on the chick's skin? To solve this mystery use a spotting scope from far away. Parent hawks will not go near the nest if they suspect it is being watched.

When

Red-tailed Hawks are diurnal, feeding during the day and resting at night.

Migration

Spring Arrival: February–April
Fall Departure: August–Nov.
They move to the southern U.S. and Mexico during the winter months. Some Red-tailed Hawks remain in Minnesota year-round.

Nesting

Red-tailed Hawks build their nests in March and April, with egg laying and incubation in April and May.

Getting Around

Red-tailed Hawks soar, perch and fly low to the ground to find prey with their keen eyesight. Once spotted, they dive or pounce on their prey, carrying it away in their strong talons. Look high in the sky for a soaring Red-tailed Hawk with its tail and wings spread out, motionless.

Where to Look

Red-tailed Hawks prefer open areas with large trees nearby but will hunt for food along roadsides in urban (city) areas also.
· Minnesota Valley Nat'l Wildlife Refuge
· Fort Snelling State Pk
· Ney Env Learning Ctr

| Year-round | Summer |
| Migration | Winter |

Ring-necked Pheasant

Phasianus colchicus

Length: 23–30 inches
Wingspan: 31 inches

female

The female is smaller than the male and brown. She blends in with the ground. Shorter, brown tail.

Red around eye

Iridescent green and purple feathers on head and neck

White collar

Long, pointed tail

A spur on back of the male's legs is for defense during territorial fights with other males

"Koork - kok!"
The male crowing,
"This is my territory."

Chinese Ring-necked Pheasant

Chinese Ring-necked Pheasant is the common name for this colorful Asian bird. Successfully introduced to Minnesota in 1916, it was a common sight in rural farming areas by the 1930s. It is one of the most popular game bird species in Minnesota (a bird that can be legally hunted for food and sport). The Minnesota DNR keeps track of the pheasant population using data gathered in an annual roadside survey. During the first two weeks in August, the DNR and volunteers survey 170 routes. Observers slowly drive a route in the early morning and record the number of pheasants they see and hear. Ask your parents and a local DNR officer if you can volunteer—be involved!

Habitat Café

Yumm . . . bring an order of seeds, grasses, leaves, roots, wild fruits, nuts and insects. Pheasants are omnivores. Females eat more insects, shells and snails during the nesting season for the calcium needed to lay eggs.

SPRING, SUMMER, FALL MENU:
Lots of seeds, some insects

WINTER MENU:
More seeds and fewer insects than during spring, summer and fall

Life Cycle

NEST The female builds the nest in tall grasses. She finds a deep spot in the ground and pulls in the grasses around her body.

EGGS About 1¾ inches long. The female incubates the 6–15 eggs for 23–25 days.

MOM! DAD! Precocial. With downy feathers, eyes open and legs well developed, the chicks follow Mom out of the nest within hours of hatching. Young pheasants are able to fly short distances by the time they are 12–14 days old.

During the first six weeks, chicks find and eat insects. What kind of insects? The largest that they can fit in their mouth and swallow! Beginning at seven weeks of age, the chicks add more plants and seeds to their diet.

JUVENILE Juvenile pheasants stay in the area with their Mom until they are 70–80 days old. The young look like adult females. Males begin to look like adults at 7–8 weeks of age. They are mature enough to date, mate, and raise their own young at one year of age.

Did You Know?

One of the most important jobs of a parent bird during incubation is turning the eggs. Eggshells have tiny holes for the exchange of air/gases and water vapor important to the developing chick. Albumin, the egg white, holds water and protein. The more albumin in the egg, the more it needs to be turned. Precocial species like pheasants that hatch with downy feathers, ready to run, have less albumin and need less egg-turning than altricial bird species, which hatch completely dependent on their parents.

When

Ring-necked Pheasants are diurnal. They feed during the day and rest at night.

Migration

Permanent resident. During the winter, flocks gather in cattail stands, grassy field edges, woodland edges and farm windbreaks to find safety from predators and blizzards. Leaving rows of corn for winter food can be helpful.

Nesting

Ring-necked Pheasants nest in May and June in Minnesota.

Getting Around

Pheasants walk and run on their powerful legs. A pheasant hidden in the grass will fly almost straight up from the ground in quick, strong bursts. Roosters may cackle as they "flush." They are short-distance flyers. At night, they roost in tree branches or nestle into stands of thick grass or cattails.

Where to Look

· Open grasslands and rural fields in the southern half of Minnesota.
· Roadside ditches, fencerows, windbreaks, pastures, hayfields and wetland edges.
· Pine to Prairie Birding Trail

Year-round	Summer
Migration	Winter

Today's Winter Special — shrub buds

Wetlands, Rivers, Lakes and Shores

Water, water, everywhere! Minnesota, the land of 10,000 lakes, provides an abundance of wet habitats for many species of birds. From the mighty Mississippi and Minnesota rivers to the prairie potholes in the southwest and Lake Superior in the northeast, birds take advantage of all the state's water.

Why Does Minnesota Have So Much Water? Fire And Ice!

We can thank volcanoes and glaciers for many of the lakes and wetlands in Minnesota. The formation of our largest body of water, Lake Superior, began with ancient volcanic activity a billion years ago. The resulting flow of lava was nearly five miles thick. The weight caused the surface of the earth to sink, leaving a depression (a very big dent in the land).

Bald Eagle

About 75,000 years ago, the Wisconsin Glacier—the last in a line of "glaciations" from the massive Laurentide Ice Sheet in Canada—moved into Minnesota. During growth spurts, it sent "lobes" of ice deep into the state. The giant glacier spun its magic over much of Minnesota, altering the landscape and leaving icy glacial meltwater that formed lakes, rivers and wetlands.

Its watery remains filled the sunken area as well, producing a huge, deep lake with rocky shores. Today, Lake Superior is important to people and birds and is a major hawk migration pathway. Check out Hawk Ridge in Duluth for a close-up view of hawk migration!

Wading Into Wetlands

Pull on your knee-high water boots and take a pal to a wetland, river or lake. They are great places to find tadpoles, giant water bugs, dragonflies, crayfish, beavers, river otters and birds. Look for the unexpected, rare animals, too. Nearly half of threatened or endangered species live in or depend on wetlands.

Wetlands are important for other reasons, too. They help filter pollutants from farm field run-off; help recharge ground water supplies; and reduce flooding, by slowing the flow of rainwater on its way to streams and rivers.

Wetlands are also a great place to have fun. People canoe, hunt, fish, explore and enjoy nature. Even though wetlands are very important places, many have been drained and filled to make way for houses, roads, stores and farmland. More

Great Egret

than half of Minnesota's original wetlands have been lost. The good news is, the DNR, conservation and sporting groups, and private citizens are working hard to protect the remaining 13.1 million acres of wetlands.

Wood Duck

Wetlands come in many shapes, types and sizes. We talk about peat bogs in the coniferous habitat section (page 26). Other wetlands are prairie potholes, shallow and deep marshes, wooded swamps, wet meadows and seasonal basins. Each kind of wetland has a special place in Minnesota's ecosystems.

Where Do Wetland Birds Live?

Just as forests have different levels that support different species of birds, a wetland, shore, lake or river has different areas, or zones, that support various plants and animals that birds use for shelter and food.

Perched on an overhanging branch, the Belted Kingfisher scans the clear, shallow water for small fish to spear. Yellow-headed Blackbirds clown around on the tops of cattails, while busy Marsh Wrens flit among the

Belted Kingfisher

cattails and reeds. Decked out in a disguise that imitates the very reeds they maneuver through, American Bitterns silently stalk small fish, crayfish, frogs and giant water beetles. Farther out on the water are colorful waterfowl—Mallards, Blue-winged Teal and Northern Shovelers.

Other waterbirds, such as Pied-billed Grebes, are out there, too, diving for fish like mini submarines. In deep, clear waters, Minnesota's majestic state bird, the Common Loon, also dives for fish. In another fascinating show, American White Pelicans herd fish into shallow waters to scoop them up in their massive bills.

Some species, such as the Red-winged Blackbird, have adapted to living along Minnesota's highways and roadways where there are cattails to perch on and insects to eat. During May and June take count of how many of the bold male Red-winged Blackbirds you can count during a road trip.

When you spot wetland birds, use these pages to check them off. The locations of these illustrations indicate where you might see them (air, water, edge or shore).

144

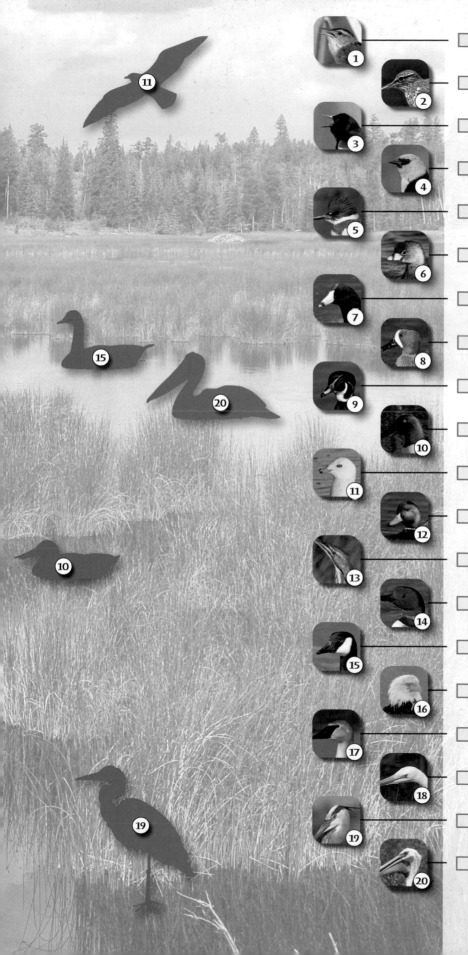

☐ Marsh Wren
(pg. 146)

☐ Spotted Sandpiper
(pg. 148)

☐ Red-winged Blackbird
(pg. 150)

☐ Yellow-headed Blackbird
(pg. 152)

☐ Belted Kingfisher
(pg. 154)

☐ Pied-billed Grebe
(pg. 156)

☐ American Coot
(pg. 158)

☐ Blue-winged Teal
(pg. 160)

☐ Wood Duck
(pg. 162)

☐ Northern Shoveler
(pg. 164)

☐ Ring-billed Gull
(pg. 166)

☐ Mallard
(pg. 168)

☐ American Bittern
(pg. 170)

☐ Common Loon
(pg. 172)

☐ Canada Goose
(pg. 174)

☐ Bald Eagle
(pg. 176)

☐ Trumpeter Swan
(pg. 178)

☐ Great Egret
(pg. 180)

☐ Great Blue Heron
(pg. 182)

☐ American White Pelican
(pg. 184)

Marsh Wren

Cistothorus palustris

Length: 4–5 inches
Wingspan: 6–7 inches

Dull black crown

White eyebrow line

Brown above, black-and-white streaked triangle on upper back

Tail has small black bars

Females and males look the same but the male is larger than the female

White underside

Males sing a song that can sound like many things, including mud bubbles popping underfoot.

Secret Agent Work Available

Zooming around in the marsh cattails like plump brown dragonflies, these tiny birds are, come a little closer, SECRETIVE. Marsh Wrens operate in disguise, camouflaged. Like their woodland cousins the House Wrens, Marsh Wren males build 2–10 houses. Why build so many basket nests among marsh cattail and reed stalks? It might be to use as decoy nests to fake out predators, or maybe apartments for young birds when they leave the parents' nest. Or could it be to show off to the gals to prove they are the big guy in the marsh? Solving the mystery of this crafty bird calls for a secret agent like you. Are those sunglasses with a detective camera in the rim? I hope they have a zoom lens!

Habitat Café

Yumm . . . bring an order of bees, wasps, ants, leafhoppers, moths, beetles and bugs. Marsh Wrens are insectivores. Scientists have observed captive Marsh Wrens dip dry food in water and soften mealworms by beating them against a perch. Do Marsh Wrens do the same in the wild? Watch close.

SPRING, SUMMER, FALL, WINTER MENU:
All insects

Today's Special
spiders

Life Cycle

NEST The female weaves wet cattail and reed leaves into a dome-shaped nest basket attached to plant stalks, 1–3 feet above water. The nest is lined with cattail down, feathers and rootlets. How do they go in and out? A hole is left in the side of the nest basket.

EGGS Almost ¾ inch long. The female incubates the clutch of 4–6 eggs for just 11–13 days.

MOM! DAD! Altricial. Hatched blind and helpless, chicks depend on Mom to feed them small insects and keep their nest clean. Dad is busy building nests and singing in a new area to try and attract another female. If he does come to the nest, the female chases him away. Why? Marsh Wrens will destroy the eggs of their own kind and other species.

NESTLING As the chicks grow in size, so, too, does the size of the insects they are fed. Mom is very busy hunting and delivering dinner!

FLEDGLING Young wrens leave the nest at 13–15 days of age. Male chicks begin learning Dad's song at 15 days.

JUVENILE Teens group together for migration. On their spring return they are mature enough to date, mate and raise their own young.

Did You Know?

Male Marsh Wrens can sing from 40 or more song patterns, sometimes even singing into the night. Why? With males competing for females, it's about setting up their home area and getting a female to come over. When a female hears a male sing, it triggers body chemicals (hormones) that tell her body it is egg-laying time. To do this she first needs a mate—the male with the finest song in the marsh!

When

Marsh Wrens are diurnal, active during the day and resting at night. Males may sing into the night, serenading Marsh Wren females and evening visitors like you!

Migration

Spring Arrival: mid-May
Fall Departure: August–October
Long-distance migrant. They migrate at night to the southern United States and Mexico.

Nesting

Marsh Wrens begin nesting in Minnesota mid-May to June.

Getting Around

Marsh Wrens move in short flights with rapid wing beats. Like acrobats on a high wire, they climb up and down cattail and reed stalks. They creep and hop along the ground, winding their way through the plants.

Where to Look

In cattail marshes all over the state, except the NE corner.
· Agassiz Env Learning Ctr and Scientific & Natural Area
· Eastside Wildlife Mgmt Area, Rochester
· McGregor Marsh, Rice Lake Nat'l Wildlife Refuge (NWR)
· Glendalough State Pk
· Pine to Prairie Birding Trail
· MN River Valley Trail
· Tamarac NWR

Year-round   Summer
Migration   Winter

Spotted Sandpiper

Actitis macularius

Length: 7–8 inches
Wingspan: 15 inches

winter

White eye-ring

Black line from bill across eye

Brown back

Long, thin orange bill with black tip

Females and males look the same

White breast and belly with black spots

Orange-pink legs

"Peet-weet." This soft call is made when flying away from danger.

Teeter-Totter Shorebirds

Up and down, teeter-totter, Spotted Sandpipers bob their tail as they pick and glean (pick up) insects, snails and crayfish along Minnesota's shorelines. The reason for the tail bobbing is a mystery. What is known, is that both chicks and adults bob their tails. At the least alarm, the motion may increase until the entire lower half of the bird's body is in a fast teeter-totter. With a little more alarm, the bird may take to the air calling, peet-weet-weet. This action by Minnesota's most common sandpiper is repeated along shorelines all over the state in spring and summer. With a buddy, binoculars and bird watching manners, explore bird playgrounds near you for teeter-tottering sandpipers!

Habitat Café

Yumm . . . bring an order of aquatic (water) and land insects, tadpoles, small frogs, mollusks and crayfish. Spotted Sandpipers are omnivorous.

SPRING, SUMMER, FALL, WINTER MENU:
🐜 Almost equal amounts of insects, amphibians and crustaceans

Today's Special
grasshoppers

Life Cycle

NEST Both parents build the 5-inch diameter nest in a shallow depression in the ground, hidden under grass or a small bush and lined with dry grass.

EGGS About 1¼ inches long. Dad is the main caregiver for the clutch of 4 eggs, which hatch in 20–21 days. A rarity in the bird world, females often mate with more than one male and lay eggs in up to five different nests.

MOM! DAD! Precocial. As soon as the chicks hatch, they walk to shore, usually with Dad—wee balls of bobbing fluff. They don't have tails at this point, just tiny rumps of fuzz. Their gray down is nearly invisible against pebbles and gravel. When in danger they flatten, becoming a part of the beach, or hurry to the water and dive for cover. One of the parents will spread its wings around the brood during the first week to keep the chicks warm and safe. They feed on insects and larvae their first day.

FLEDGLING Flight becomes routine when they are just weeks old.

JUVENILE At one year of age the birds are mature enough to date, mate and raise their own young.

Did You Know?

Spotted Sandpipers change their fashion each season. Just before fall migration, Spotted Sandpipers become UNspotted. They molt, or lose their old feathers and grow in new white feathers without spots. Their bill and legs turn to a dull yellow color during the winter. When it is time for spring and the nesting season to begin, they molt into spotted feathers again!

When

Spotted Sandpipers are diurnal. They feed during the day and rest at night.

Migration

Spring Arrival: mid April
Fall Departure: August–Sept.
Long-distance migrant. Solitary (alone) bird, even in migration. Migrates by night to wintering areas in southern U.S. and as far south as Bolivia and Brazil.

Nesting

Spotted Sandpipers nest in late May–June in Minnesota.

Getting Around

Spotted Sandpipers fly directly up from shore in a burst of take-off energy. In flight, their wings are stiff and flap only halfway up. This gives them a short, flickering style of flight. Look for the white wing bars in flight. They dive straight into the water for safety and then straight out again from underneath the water!

Where to Look

Spotted Sandpipers live all over Minnesota along the shorelines of lakes, ponds, streams, rivers and wetlands. They use dry grassy lands nearby for nesting and perch on fence posts.

Year-round	Summer
Migration	Winter

Red-winged Blackbird

Agelaius phoeniceus

Length: 7–9 inches
Wingspan: 13 inches

Males are glossy black

female

Females have a light eyebrow stripe. They are brown above with streaks of brown below.

Red shoulder patch with a yellow border

It takes young males two years to become black like Dad—called "delayed maturation"

"O-ka-leee!" means "Guys, stay away from my territory! But gals come on over—I have room for 3 or 4."

Safety in Numbers

Red-winged Blackbirds take safety in numbers to the max. (It's harder for predators to capture prey in a large group.) In late summer, redwings attend the annual family reunion with their cousins: starlings, grackles and cowbirds. Look for a flying river of blackbirds above the fields and across the sky at dawn and dusk in September and October. It can take more than 10 minutes for a massive flock of 10,000 birds to pass. Flocks feed in the fields during the day and roost at night. Female redwings migrate south in the fall before males. In the spring, males return first to Minnesota's wetlands and roadsides to perch on a cattail, spread their red wing patches, and sing "O-ka-lee . . . ."

Habitat Café

Yumm . . . bring an order of dragonflies, grasshoppers, spiders, beetles, moths and seeds like sunflowers. Their slender brown bill is designed to pick up insects and seeds. Red-winged Blackbirds are omnivorous.

SPRING, SUMMER MENU:
Mainly insects, some seeds and berries

FALL, WINTER MENU:
More seeds and berries, fewer insects than during spring and summer

Today's Special
snails

Life Cycle

NEST The female builds the nest cup 3–10 feet above the ground in cattails, reeds and bushes over or near water. She weaves the leaves of water plants through the cattail stalks to make a nest cup. The inside of the nest is lined with soft, fine grasses.

EGGS About 1 inch long. The female incubates the 3–4 blue-green eggs with brown markings for 11 days.

MOM! DAD! Altricial. The female feeds the young and removes the fecal sacs (chick diapers) from the nest. If a predator comes too close to the nest, the female does a "flip-wing act" 5–10 feet from the nest.

NESTLING The chicks' eyes open when they are six days old.

FLEDGLING Both parents feed the young for up to two weeks after they leave the nest.

JUVENILE Juveniles join a flock with other "teens." They feed during the day and roost at night. By fall they join a large group of both males and females, and prepare to migrate to wintering areas.

Do the Math

Red-winged Blackbird chicks are fed insects. Insects are much higher in muscle and bone-building protein than seeds and berries. A male chick will increase in size by ten times in its first ten days. Multiply your birth weight by ten and you would be HUGE in only ten days. Do the math! But then, you don't need to grow into an adult your first year like a Red-winged Blackbird does. Answer on pages 194-195.

When

Red-winged Blackbirds are diurnal. They feed during the day and rest at night.

Migration

Spring Arrival: March–April
Fall Departure: October–Nov.
Long-distance migrant. Red-winged Blackbirds gather in large groups of up to 100,000 birds before migrating to the southern U.S. and as far as Mexico and South America.

Nesting

Red-winged Blackbirds nest in Minnesota during May and June.

Getting Around

Look for Minnesota's most common summer roadside bird sitting on top of signs, mile markers and fence posts. They walk on the ground to search for seeds and insects. Redwings fly in a pattern of closing their wings, dipping down, then rising again with a few wing beats.

Where to Look

Red-winged Blackbirds are found in most of Minnesota where there is water. Look for them in wet roadsides and fields, marshes and along the reedy edges of lakes.
· A *Super Adaptor*

Year-round	Summer
Migration	Winter

Yellow-headed Blackbird

Xanthocephalus xanthocephalus

Length: 8–11 inches
Wingspan: 15 inches

female

Male wears all black with a bright yellow head and breast

Females are smaller than males. They are brown with a pale yellow throat and eyebrow stripe. No white wing patch, but they have white spots on the chest.

White wing patches

Long black tail

"Kuk-koh-koh-koh—waaaaaa!"
Males saying,
"This is my space.
Females are welcome."

Clowns of the Cattails

Clowning around in their bright yellow hoods and white wing patches, male Yellow-headed Blackbirds add humor to a marsh. Perched on top of a cattail or reed, a male spreads his tail wide, twists his neck, and turns his head toward the open sky to swell his sunny throat with an unborn song. With such great effort, one expects a song that matches the brilliant colors of summer. Instead, these fellows sound as if they are choking on an angry dragonfly while squealing a series of painful hiccups. Get a marsh full of males performing this act and the cattail arena is a circus of clowns!

Habitat Café

Yumm . . . bring an order of dragonflies, beetles, waterbugs and weed and grain crop seeds. Their long, pointed bill pokes cattail heads for insect larvae and snatches flying insects. Yellow-headed Blackbirds are omnivorous.

SPRING MENU:
Mainly aquatic insects, some seeds

SUMMER, FALL, WINTER MENU:
Almost all seeds, a few insects

Today's Special
snails

Life Cycle

NEST The female weaves the basket-like nest at least 2–4 feet above water. It is attached to plant stems with wet leaves. When the nest dries, it shrinks and is very tight on the plant supports. The nest is lined with soft, dry weed leaves and the fluffy down of last year's cattail heads.

 EGGS About 1 inch long. The female incubates the clutch of 3–5 eggs for 12–14 days.

MOM! DAD! Altricial. Mom feeds the chicks and does diaper duty (removes fecal sacs). Dad is busy with 2–3 families and brings food to the nest at times.

NESTLING The chicks that beg the loudest get food first.

FLEDGLING Perched at the rim of the nest, 9- to 12-day-old chicks leap off and land in the plants nearby. For the first few days out of the nest, the parents bring food to the young. They can fly at 3 weeks of age.

JUVENILE In late July to September, both adult and immature Yellow-headed Blackbirds group in flocks in thick stands of cattails and rushes. They are mature enough to raise their own families in the spring.

Do the Math

Cattails have parachute-like seeds that can travel with the wind up to 100 miles. There can be 300,000 seeds packed into just one cattail head. That's enough seeds to plant 6 acres of marsh. If an acre of cattails has 1,000 cattail heads, how many seeds could be parachuting in the air when the heads burst in the autumn? Do the math! Answer on pages 194-195.

When

Yellow-headed Blackbirds are diurnal. They feed during the day and rest at night.

Migration

Spring Arrival: mid-April–May
Fall Departure: October
Short- to long-distance migrant to the southern United States and Mexico.

Nesting

Yellow-headed Blackbirds nest in colonies beginning mid-May–June in Minnesota.

Getting Around

Yellow-headed Blackbirds hop and walk when foraging on the ground. These wetland clowns will also climb up and then slide down vertical plant stems! Their flight is undulating (up and down) with the tail held out behind the body.

Where to Look

Watch for Yellow-headed Blackbirds in wetlands, marshes and around the edges of lakes and rivers. It generally prefers marshes with deeper water than those favored by its cousin the Red-winged Blackbird.
· Agassiz Nat'l Wildlife Refuge
· Big Stone Nat'l Wildlife Refuge
· Tamarac Nat'l Wildlife Refuge
· Swan Lake in Nicollet County

Year-round	Summer
Migration	Winter

Belted Kingfisher

Ceryle alcyon

Length: 11–14 inches
Wingspan: 20 inches

Head crest can stick straight up or stay closer to the head

female

Females wear a rusty-orange-colored belt

Juveniles look like adults but with a much smaller bill

Blue-gray above with a white throat collar and a blue band across the chest

Males do not have a belt

"Rattle, rattle, rattle..." This rattle call echoes against stream banks and riverbanks.

Expert Anglers

Scan the telephone wires and tree branches over a stream or river for the big-crested head and broad bill of this expert angler. Then sit quietly and watch as the blue-gray kingfisher studies the shallow, clear water for the movement of small fish, frogs and crayfish. Once it spots dinner, it dives like an arrow, plunging its bill into the water. Captured! The prey is taken back to the perch where the kingfisher shakes its head and pounds the fish. This stuns the fish, breaks up the bones of sticklebacks and bullheads, and turns the fish around for swallowing headfirst. The kingfisher's two-part stomach is not equipped for scales and bones. Instead, these hard-to-digest items are formed into a pellet and coughed up.

Habitat Café

Yumm . . . bring an order of tadpoles, small fish, crayfish and dragonflies. Belted Kingfishers are carnivorous. They most often eat small fish that live in shallow water or stay near the surface. A Kingfisher uses its thick pincher bill to catch prey. Look for its white wing patches in flight.

SPRING, SUMMER, FALL, WINTER MENU:
Fish, frogs, tadpoles and aquatic insects

Today's Special
Leopard
Frogs

Life Cycle

NEST Both male and female dig out a tunnel just a few feet from the top of a river or stream bank, sand or gravel pit, or bluff. At the end of the 3- to 15-foot tunnel is a nesting room. The eggs are laid on fish bones and scales from spit-up food pellets that have fallen apart.

EGGS Slightly more than 1¼ inches long. The female incubates the clutch of 6–7 eggs for 22–24 days. Dad sits in when Mom takes a break.

MOM! DAD! Altricial. Both parents bring a wad of regurgitated fish to feed the chicks during the first days. Dad does more of the fishing, bringing back whole fish as the young grow.

NESTLING More like a cat in a litter box than a bird, nestlings back up and shoot their feces on the wall. They turn around and with their bill, hammer soil from the wall over the top of it.

FLEDGLING At 27–29 days of age, Mom or Dad sits on a nearby perch with a fish in its bill. When the chicks are hungry enough, they come out. Parents feed them in decreasing amounts for another three weeks.

JUVENILE Teens take ten days of fishing lessons. Their parents drop dead fish in the water and they capture it.

Unsolved Mystery

What kind of fish did the kingfisher eat for dinner last week? To solve this mystery, first find their perch and look underneath for pellets. Inside the pellets are the answers to their recent menu. You may find bones and scales that will help you identify the species of fish they ate. You can even tell how old the fish were by counting the rings on the scales!

When

Kingfishers are diurnal. They feed during the day and rest at night.

Migration

Spring Arrival: March–April Fall Departure: Oct.–Nov. Short- to long-distance migrant to as far as Central or South America.

Nesting

They dig out the nest burrow in April with incubation in May in Minnesota.

Getting Around

Kingfishers perch on a branch, rock outcrop or on a wire over a river, stream or lake. Once they spot prey, they dive headfirst, catching it in their large bill. They also hover over an area for a short time to catch prey. Their short legs and feet with joined toes are not adapted for walking. They only need their feet for shuffling in and out of their burrow and for perching.

Where to Look

Along Minnesota's streams, rivers and lakes.
· Root River State Trail
· Great River Birding Trail
· Minnesota River Valley Birding Trail
· St. Croix River
· Pine to Prairie Birding Trail

Year-round	Summer
Migration	Winter

Pied-billed Grebe

Podilymbus podiceps

Length: 12–15 inches
Wingspan: 16 inches

juvenile

winter

White eye-rings look like sunglasses with a fake nose

Square-ish, flat head

Dark brown all over with a white patch underneath

White bill with a black ring around the middle

Flat, green, partially webbed (lobed) toes and feet

Females and males look similar. Males are larger.

"Kuk-kuk-kuk-kuk-kuk-kuk-kuk, cow-cow-uh, cow-uh, cow-uh-cow-uh." Call begins soft and slow but ends loud and fast.

Mini-submarines of the Marsh

Where did it go? Sinking in the water like a sneaky mini-submarine, a Pied-billed Grebe can keep you waiting for its return. With their periscope eyes and nostrils the only parts above water, they can stay hidden for a long time. By forcing out the air held in their feathers and body, they sink in the water to watch for predators. Cloaked in disguise, their banded black-and-white bill looks like the rippled surface of the water. Built for diving, their legs are far back on their body and their wings are small. But, don't let their small size fool you. They can sneak up on other birds in fierce attacks that claim their territory and protect their young. There it is—gone again!

Habitat Café

Yumm . . . bring an order of fish, dragonflies and nymphs, beetles, bugs, snails, mussels, frogs and crayfish. Their chicken-like, arched bill is just right for catching prey or crushing crustaceans. Pied-billed Grebes are both insectivores and carnivores.

SPRING, SUMMER, FALL, WINTER MENU:
Equal amounts of fish and insects, some crustaceans

Today's Special
feathers

Life Cycle

NEST As soon as the winter ice is melted, the female and male build their nest on a floating mat of decayed vegetation held to plant stalks in water at least one foot deep.

 EGGS About 1¾ inches long. The female incubates the clutch of 4–8 eggs for just 23 days. She covers the eggs with a layer of plant leaves when she takes a break.

MOM! DAD! Precocial. Chicks can leave the nest for brief periods as soon as they are dry. They are in danger of drowning so they hitch a ride on the back of Mom and Dad. This cozy ride also protects them from predators.

In only a few weeks, these little black-and-white striped "water skunks" can swim, dive and sink like their parents.

FLEDGLING The young grebes are able to fly and become independent when they are 8–9 weeks of age.

JUVENILE On their spring migration return, they are mature enough to date, mate and raise their own young.

Gross Factor

Grebes eat their own feathers throughout their lifetime, filling nearly half their stomach capacity at times. Parents feed feathers to their chicks soon after hatching. Biologists theorize that the feathers act to strain the stomach contents, preventing fish bones from passing into the intestines. Periodically, grebes spit up pellets of undigested feathers and other hard matter. Gross!

When
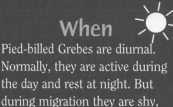
Pied-billed Grebes are diurnal. Normally, they are active during the day and rest at night. But during migration they are shy, nighttime fliers.

Migration
Spring Arrival: April
Fall Departure: Oct.–Nov.
Long-distance migrant wintering in the southern United States and Mexico.

Nesting
Pied billed Grebes begin nesting in Minnesota as soon as the winter ice is melted—in late April and May.

Getting Around
Being wary birds, Pied-billed Grebes crash-dive into the water when they sense danger. This causes a spray of water several feet into the air, blocking the vision of the predator. By the time the spray is gone, so, too, is the sneaky grebe!

Where to Look
Pied-billed Grebes are common summertime sights in wetlands, shallow lakes and ponds that have dense stands of cattails and open water. Watch for grebes diving for small fish, insects and crustaceans.

Year-round	Summer
Migration	Winter

American Coot

Fulica americana

Length: 13–16 inches
Wingspan: 24 inches

diving

White forehead shield with bright red spot

Red eyes

Chicken-like white bill with black ring

Black all over

Stubby, upturned tail

Nickname: Mud Hen

Green-lobed toes and green legs

Females and males look alike

"Kuk-kuk-kuk!" means "This is my territory!"

Dare to be Different

Coots dream to be ducks. They are, however, in the rail bird family. Most rails spend their time wading along shores. Not the coot. Coots want it both ways, shorebird and duck. It appears that their dream has come true, or nearly so. Their body shape is flat, like a duck. Dense (thickly spaced) feathers on their underside are made for being in the water, like a duck. To get around on both land and water, their green feet are partly webbed, called lobed. Where did the interesting chicken-like bill come from? That remains a mystery. American Coots are a bit like the comical flip books that combine different body parts to make a truly one-of-a-kind combination!

Habitat Café

Yumm . . . bring an order of aquatic insects, worms, tadpoles, snails and crayfish during breeding season. During non-breeding season bring an order of aquatic seeds, plant tubers and leaves. American Coots are omnivorous.

Today's Special
wild rice

SPRING, SUMMER MENU:
🌱 Plant matter, with equal amounts of insects and crustaceans on the side

FALL, WINTER MENU:
🌱 Mostly plant matter, some insects and crustaceans

Life Cycle

NEST The female builds the floating nest of plant leaves attached a few inches above the water to cattail and reed stalks. The nest is hidden in the edges of shallow lakes, ponds and wetlands.

EGGS About 2 inches long. Dad incubates the clutch of 6–12 eggs for 22–24 days. Mom pitches in at times.

MOM! DAD! Precocial. The black, downy chicks leave the nest soon after their down is dry. Frosted with white and wearing bright red patches on their head, the chicks could be in a Dr. Suess book!

Dad builds a brooding platform on a muskrat house, a mat of floating plants or a repaired nest. When the chicks are cold from the night air or storms, Dad or Mom keep them warm on the platform.

The chicks are fed insects during the first weeks by their parents. They feed themselves at 4–5 weeks of age. They add plants to their diet.

JUVENILE Juveniles leave the family group to join a flock of coots. When they are three months of age, they have grown to adult size.

Did You Know?

How many eyelids do birds have? Three. They have an upper and lower lid and a third, usually clear lid between the two lids and the cornea. The third lid is the nictitating membrane. This lid is used for blinking and keeps their eyes clean, moist and protected from their chicks while they feed them. In loons and other diving birds, the nictitating membrane has a clear center, which acts like a contact lens underwater.

When ☀

America Coots are diurnal. They feed during the day and rest at night.

Migration

Spring Arrival: March–April
Fall Departure: October–Nov. Long-distance migrant. In the fall, they fly by night to winter in the southern U.S., Mexico and at times, Central America.

Nesting

American Coots nest in Minnesota during May–June. They may have more than one brood per season.

Getting Around

Looking like a child's small pull-toy, coots nod their heads in time with their feet and tail both on land and in the water. Like many diving birds, their bones are solid rather than semi-hollow and their legs are positioned far back on their body. Solid bones give them the extra weight they need to dive fast and deep. Their legs may help them swim and dive, but their design makes for clumsy take-offs from the water.

Where to Look

American Coots live in marshes and reedy lakes statewide.

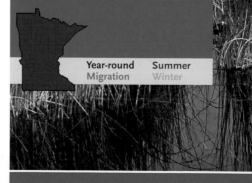

Year-round	Summer
Migration	Winter

Blue-winged Teal

Anas discors

Length: 14–16 inches
Wingspan: 23 inches

male

Look for blue wing
patches and white
wing bars

female

In flight, the top of
wings are blue, white
and green with a
brown outer half

Males have a
blue-gray head

A white, half-moon
crescent between
the bill and eye

White wing bars

Females are brown with a
faint white patch at the
base of their bill. No white
band on forewing.

Orange legs
and feet

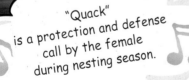
"Quack"
is a protection and defense
call by the female
during nesting season.

Dabblers

Is the duck stuck? No, the bird with its rump sticking up from the water is a dabbling duck. There are two groups of ducks: dabblers and divers. Dabbling ducks tip up as they reach down through the water with their bill and neck to forage for plant and animal food on the pond bottom. This is called dabbling. Just under the water, their feet paddle to keep them partly under. Blue-winged Teal and Mallards are dabblers. They live in shallow water. Diving ducks live in deep water and have small wings, square heads, legs located far back on their body, and swim low in the water. Whether you are watching dabblers or divers, it is certain that you are dabbling in a super way to spend a day!

Habitat Café

Yumm . . . bring an order of insects, larvae and worms during the spring breeding season. In late summer through the winter months, soft plant parts, wild rice, grasses, sedges and pondweeds. Blue-winged Teals are omnivorous.

Today's Special
tadpoles

SPRING, SUMMER, FALL MENU:
Mostly insects and larvae, some seeds

WINTER MENU:
Lots of seeds, some insects

Life Cycle

NEST The female weaves cattail leaves and dry grasses into a basket-like nest on dry ground near water. She lines the nest with her down feathers and arches nearby grasses over the top, making the nest nearly invisible.

EGGS About 1¾ inches long. The female incubates the clutch of 8–13 white eggs for 21–24 days.

MOM! DAD! Precocial. Soon after hatching, Mom leads the downy ducklings from the nest to water. They do not come back to the nest but for the first two weeks, Mom does brood them on chilly nights. The ducklings find insects on land and water on their own.

FLEDGLING Early nesters due to late spring arrival and early fall migration departure, Blue-winged Teals mature very quickly. The young take flight at 40 days of age.

JUVENILE Mom goes her own way and the teens prepare for fall migration. When they return in the spring they are mature enough to date, mate and raise their own young.

Did You Know?

A migrating bird is busy with 4–5 major events in a year. Each event has to follow in order for the bird to survive. Between spring and fall flights, they have a breeding season and one or two molting periods. A female Blue-winged Teal must molt her feathers between the time she finishes her parent duties and fall migration. Birds generally do not migrate with missing feathers. Males molt earlier and migrate south before females.

When
Blue-winged Teal are diurnal, active during the day and resting at night.

Migration
Spring Arrival: April
Fall Departure: September
Long-distance migrant. Blue-winged Teals are among the first waterfowl to leave Minnesota in the fall and the last to return in spring from wintering grounds in the southern United States through South America, including Brazil and central Chile. They fly in small flocks of 10–40 birds.

Nesting
Blue-winged Teal begin nesting in late May–June in Minnesota.

Getting Around
Blue-winged Teal move in an instant, taking flight straight off from the water! They often fly at speeds of 30–50 miles per hour, and can hit 60 during migration flight.

Where to Look
Watch for Blue-winged Teal in Minnesota's shallow marshes, ponds and mud flats near land with an abundance of short- and medium-height grasses which can be used for nesting.

Year-round	Summer
Migration	Winter

Wood Duck

Aix sponsa

Length: 17–19 inches
Wingspan: 30 inches

female

Female is brown. Breast white streaked above, gray below. White eye patch. White throat. Bushy, pointed crest.

Red eye and eye-ring

Yellow and red bill with a black tip

Iridescent green head and slicked back crest

Long, dark tail held at upright angle

White throat, chin collar and strap

"Jeeb!" is a whistle made by male Wood Ducks. Females call "Oo-eek, oo-eek" to their broods, and often give the call while in flight.

Another Minnesota Success Story

Wood Ducks need habitat. They need old trees with holes for nesting, plus food, shelter and nearby water. Drain wetland habitat, harvest older woodland trees and hunt more ducks than can be hatched and raised each year and Wood Ducks become rare. By 1920, this was the case in Minnesota. The good news is that wildlife biologists studied the needs of Wood Ducks and came up with a plan. Nest boxes were built and placed near wetlands, lakes and rivers. The biologists kept track of the boxes and recorded the data. The number of Wood Ducks hunters were allowed to harvest each year was closely regulated. The plan worked. Today, Wood Ducks are all over the state. Success happens.

Habitat Café

Yumm . . . bring an order of seeds and tender shoots of aquatic (water) plants, fruit and nuts, insects and snails. Wood Ducks have a stretchy esophagus to store food for eating later. One duck had 30 acorns stored in its esophagus! Wood Ducks are omnivorous.

SPRING, SUMMER, FALL MENU:
Almost entirely plant matter, some animal matter

WINTER MENU:
Mostly seeds and acorns, more animal matter than summer

Today's Special
acorns and dragonflies

Life Cycle

NEST The female makes the nest in a tree cavity or woodpecker hole, 6–30 feet above ground and near a wetland, small lake or river. She lines the nest with her down feathers. Wood Ducks will also use a nest box lined with wood chips.

EGGS About 2 inches long. The female incubates the clutch of 10–15 eggs for 25–35 days. Sometimes, several females will all lay 30–40 eggs in just ONE nest box. One lucky hen will incubate all of the eggs!

MOM! DAD! Precocial. Hatched with eyes open, with warm brown and yellow down and sharp toenails. After a day of fluffing out, they climb to the edge of the nesting hole, pop out and float to the ground. Mom calls an O.K. signal, "kuk, kuk, kuk" and watches without helping. She leads her waddling puffballs to the nearest water. Mom keeps them warm at night for the first month. Young birds are able to fly and become independent at 7–10 weeks old.

JUVENILE Juveniles group in late summer to early fall. A female picks her mate on the southern wintering grounds. The chosen male follows her back to her original nesting area to make their new home.

Birding Tip

You can build a nesting box, too! Place your box in Wood Duck habitat, check it regularly and then record the data during the nesting season. The hens do not mind an occasional visit to peek inside. If you get up early on the day after hatching, you might be able to count the chicks that pop out of the nest and float to the ground!

When

Wood Ducks are diurnal. They feed during the day and rest at night.

Migration
Spring Arrival: March
Fall Departure: October
Long-distance migrant. Winter in the southern United States and Mexico. A few hardy Wood Ducks may overwinter in southeastern Minnesota.

Nesting
Wood Ducks nest in late May– early June in Minnesota. Use nest boxes or natural tree cavities near water.

Getting Around
Wood Ducks fly straight and fast into their nesting hole—without bumping their head! They walk along the water's edge to feed. In the water, they are excellent swimmers. They dive to escape predators. Take-off from the water is quick and straight up with very fast wing beats.

Where to Look
Wooded habitat along rivers, streams and small lakes across most of Minnesota.
· Upper Miss. Nat'l Wildlife Refuge
· Great River Birding Trail
· Richardson Nature Ctr
· Whitewater Wildlife Mgmt Area
· Hyland Park Reserve
· Carlos Avery Wildlife Mgmt Area

Year-round	**Summer**
Migration	Winter

Northern Shoveler

Anas clypeata

Length: 17–20 inches
Wingspan: 27–33 inches

female

Females are mottled brown. Their bill is dark with orange.

Black head glossed with iridescent green

This dabbling duck has a one-of-a-kind shovel-like bill

Large pale-blue wing patch

White breast

Male's "took, took, took" means "I'm here!"

The Whirlpool Effect

Bottoms up! A shoveler points its tail to the sky and reaches down with its long neck to strain aquatic plants and small animals from the water, with the help of its spoon-shaped bill. (The tip is two times as wide as the base.) Shovelers also hunt in groups. With buddies, they form a tight circle and follow the leader around and around until a spinning whirlpool brings food from the marsh bottom to the water's surface. Shovelers have a system of lamellae, comb-like teeth, along the edges of their bill that act like a strainer to catch tiny food prey. They draw water through their bill and pump it out the sides with their tongue, draining the water while keeping in the food. Yum!

Habitat Café

Yumm . . . bring an order of diatoms, ostracods, copepods (microscopic water animals), snails, dragonfly nymphs and caddis fly larvae from the surface and muddy bottoms of lakes, streams and wetlands. Northern Shovelers are omnivorous. They eat plant and animal matter.

SPRING, SUMMER, FALL MENU:
Lots of seeds and leaves of water plants, some small water animals

Today's Special
water boatmen

Life Cycle

NEST The female builds the grassy nest bowl by shallow marshes in an open space on the ground. She lines the nest with her down feathers.

EGGS About 2 inches long. The female incubates the clutch of 8–12 eggs for 21–26 days.

MOM! DAD! Precocial and downy. Within 24 hours after hatching, Mom leads the dark brown and white-and-yellow downy ducklings to water. Dad is off on his own, feeding and molting his feathers. A diet of small insects and crustaceans provides the protein the young birds need to keep up with their fast growth.

FLEDGLING By the time the chicks are two weeks old, their bill has taken on the family trait of a spoon and shovel ready for use. They dive and begin to fly on their own when they are 6–8 weeks of age.

JUVENILE Immature Northern Shovelers return to Minnesota the next spring mature enough to mate and raise their own young.

Did You Know?

How does a duck stay warm and dry while in the water? Oil. Above the bird's tail is a gland that holds oil, called the uropygial gland. The duck reaches back with its bill to collect the oil and then spreads it over its feathers while preening. The oil makes a waterproof seal and worries of getting wet slide away like water over a duck!

When
Northern Shovelers are diurnal, active during the day and resting at night.

Migration
Spring Arrival: March–April
Fall Departure: October
Long-distance migrant. Flies during the day to wintering areas in the southern United States and Mexico.

Nesting
Northern Shovelers begin nesting in late May–early June in Minnesota.

Getting Around
Northern Shovelers sit low in shallow water where they dabble for their dinner. Their flight is direct, steady and slow. Males will perform a flight display where they burst into a fast flight and dash through the air in an attempt to impress a female—and probably you, too!

Where to Look
Marshes, the edges of shallow lakes, and in the slow-flowing muddy waters of creeks and rivers are all excellent places to look for Northern Shovelers. Explore the shallow wetlands along the Minnesota and Mississippi rivers in Minnesota.

Year-round	Summer
Migration	Winter

Ring-billed Gull

Larus delawarensis

Length: 18–20 inches
Wingspan: 4 feet

immature

winter

Yellow bill with
a black "ring"
near the tip

Gray wings

Look for black
wing tips with
white spots

White body

Yellow legs
and feet

Females and males
look the same

*"Keeeeeaaaah—
kah,kah,kah,kah,kah!"*

First-Come, First-Served

Ring-billed Gulls are taking over the nesting grounds of Common Terns, long-time residents of Leech Lake in Cass County, Minnesota. Why? Ring-billed Gulls are pushy when staking their claim to habitat. On a first-come, first-served basis, gulls arrive on the spring nesting grounds a few weeks before Common Terns. Gulls do not depend on open water to find food; they are scavengers, eating anything edible. Common Terns eat fish and need open water. Bewildered, they come home after the ice has melted to find their shores occupied by gulls. Common Terns are losing ground on the shores of Leech Lake to Ring-billed Gulls that can chow on almost anything—including your leftover peanut butter.

Habitat Café

Yumm . . . bring an order of fish, insects, spiders, earthworms and waste grains (corn). Ring-billed Gulls are omnivorous. They eat both plant and animal matter.

SPRING, SUMMER, FALL, WINTER MENU:
Animal and plant matter

Today's Special
human food garbage

Life Cycle

NEST The nest is on a beach or island in the open ground on matted plants or in rocks. Champion recyclers, they may even line their nest with garbage.

no photo available

EGGS Slightly more than 2¼ inches long. The female incubates the clutch of 2–3 eggs for 20–23 days.

MOM! DAD! Semi-precocial. Chicks blend into the shore with mottled brown, gray or white down on their backs and white bellies. They eat food that their parents ate and then spit up near the nest. Sometimes they get fly-up delivery and are able to take the food right out of their parent's mouth as it comes up. Scrumptious!

NESTLING Chicks can swim at 2–3 days of age. With so many adults in a gull colony, which two birds are Mom and Dad? Chicks know their own parents' calls when they are 4–5 days of age.

FLEDGLING Young birds fledge when they are 20–40 days of age and leave the family group when they are able to fly at 5 weeks.

JUVENILE The ring on their bill develops at one year of age and adult plumage at three years of age.

Unsolved Mystery

Do birds play or are all their actions related to survival? Watch gulls as they drop an object and then swoop down to pick it up, drop the object and swoop to pick it up, drop the object...over and over. Are they in practice for catching prey, or playing a game for fun? This unsolved mystery can play with your ability to catch the clues and pick up a winning answer!

When
Ring-billed Gulls are diurnal, active during the day and resting at night.

Migration
Spring Arrival: late March–April
Fall Departure: Sept.–Nov.
Short-distance migrant to lakes, rivers, landfills, golf courses, fields and parks in the southern U.S. and northern Mexico.

Nesting
In Minnesota, Ring-billed Gulls begin nesting in colonies in May.

Getting Around
Ring-billed Gulls walk along a shore in a side-to-side stride with attitude! Look for their wings held in a V-shape as they land on water. Floating atop the water like a buoy, they dip their head under for food. In the air, they are strong fliers that can also hover and soar on thermals.

Where to Look
Ring-billed Gulls prefer islands, rock reefs and marshes. Adapted to living near people.
· Grassy Point/Duluth Harbor
· St. Louis River area
· Duluth-Superior Harbor
· Mille Lacs Lake
· Leech Lake
· North Shore, Lake Superior

Year-round	Summer
Migration	Winter

Mallard

Anas platyrhynchos

Length: 20–27 inches
Wingspan: 35 inches

male tail curl

female

Male (drake) has a green head with a white neck ring and a red-brown chest

Male has a black tail curl

Females, or hens, are streaked brown. Orange bill with small black spots. The speculum, a band of wing color, is metallic blue edged with white.

Orange, webbed feet paddle water and push the body down to reach plants

"Quack, quack" is made only by females. Males have two calls of their own, a nasal warning "rhaeb" and a short courtship whistle.

From Marshes to Malls—Mallards Are All Over Minnesota!

Mallards are *Super Adaptors*. In the Twin Cities, they have been seen nesting in flower planters in mall parking lots and in large flowerpots on 17th-floor balconies of buildings! Close to people or not, as long as there is shallow water and food near, Mallards are content. They eat everything from insects to frogs, plants that live under and on top of water, seeds from farm crops and wild plants. Watch for Mallards eating cracked corn under bird feeders. Mallards are also big eaters of mosquito larvae and pupae that live on the top of shallow water. With Mallards near, you can enjoy being outdoors with fewer mosquitoes to swat. Besides, Mallards smell better than insect repellent!

Habitat Café

Today's Special
wild rice
and corn

Yumm . . . bring an order of seeds and shoots of aquatic plants, grass, snails, worms and insects. Mallards are omnivorous. They eat both plant and animal matter, depending on the season.

SPRING BREEDING SEASON MENU:
Lots of insects and animal matter

SPRING, SUMMER, FALL MENU:
Includes aquatic plants and seeds

WINTER MENU:
Can include grains from farm crops

Life Cycle

NEST Built near water at the base of tall wetland plants or under a woody shrub. The female makes a few scrapes in the ground and lays her eggs. She then adds grass, reeds and leaves from nearby plants to make a nest rim around her body. Soft down feathers line the inside.

EGGS About 2¼ inches long. The female incubates the clutch of 9–13 eggs for 26–30 days.

MOM! DAD! Precocial. Mallard ducklings hatch covered with fluffy down and their eyes fully open. Mom is on her own with her large brood. The hatchlings are out of the nest after the first day and follow her to water.

Mallards dive for food during the first weeks after hatching, but this behavior all but disappears with the arrival of their flight feathers. Until they can fly at two months of age, they still need Mom's protection from snapping turtles, bass and raccoons.

JUVENILE At 10 weeks of age, young Mallards leave the family group to join a mixed flock of adults and juveniles. When they return in the spring, they are mature enough to raise their own family.

Did You Know?

While Mom is taking care of the ducklings, Dad joins a flock and stays very quiet. Male mallards molt, or lose the old feathers and grow new ones, before fall migration. The bright breeding season feathers are replaced by dull camouflaged brown feathers called "eclipse plumage." During this time, they are unable to fly for a short period until the new feathers grow in.

When
Diurnal. They feed during the day and rest at night.

Migration
Spring Arrival: mid-March
Fall Departure: November
Long-distance migrant to the southern United States and Mexico. Some Mallards stay in Minnesota during the winter, wherever they find suitable open water within a reasonable "commuting distance" of feeding areas.

Nesting
Nest in Minnesota during May–June.

Getting Around
Mallards are strong and direct fliers capable of reaching speeds up to 45–60 miles per hour. When they are alarmed they can spring straight up from the water. They use their wings and feet as brakes when making a landing into water! Mallards are also excellent swimmers.

Where to Look
Lakes, wetlands, rivers, parks and farm ponds. Explore city, county and state parks, and public areas or nature centers. Mallards may even eat cracked corn under bird feeders!
· A *Super Adaptor*

Year-round	Summer
Migration	Winter

American Bittern

Botaurus lentiginosus

Length: 23–27 inches
Wingspan: 3–4 feet

Yellow eyes on the side of their head

Long dark patch from eye down side of neck

Short, white neck with brown streaks that look like dry marsh grass

Compact, plump brown body

Adult females and males look the same. Males are a bit larger.

"Oon-ka-chuun-K!" means "Stay away, fellas—this is my space. Ladies, come over to my marsh-pad!"

Short, yellow-green legs and feet with very long toes

Oon-ka-chuun-K, oon-ka-chuun-K

Strange noises come from Minnesota's marshes. "Oon-ka-chuun-K," it echoes. The deep thumps and ka-chunks of American Bitterns sound like the pumping of a giant hobgoblin. Look in the marsh for a big blade of grass moving in the wind. Look closer. Stretching its white-and-brown neck to the sky, an American Bittern sways back and forth like pretend grass in the wind. The strange sound starts as the bird fills its esophagus like a balloon. Once the area is closed, like tying the balloon shut, it works like a drum. The sound from the vocal cords bounces off the balloon-sac, making it louder. The bittern's body and neck stay blown out until the very end, making the last metallic note, "K," very loud.

Habitat Café

Yumm . . . bring an order of dragonflies, other insects, crawfish, frogs, mice, small fish and lizards. American Bitterns are carnivorous. They eat only animal matter found around their marshy habitat.

SPRING, SUMMER, FALL, WINTER MENU:
Mostly insects, some amphibians, reptiles, mammals and crustaceans

oday's Special
small snakes

Life Cycle

NEST The female builds a grassy nest on the ground or short mound hidden in the thick marsh plants.

EGGS About 2 inches long. The female incubates the clutch of 4–5 eggs for 24–28 days.

MOM! DAD! Altricial. Mom is the sole parent in this family, feeding and caring for the chicks.

NESTLING The downy, funny-looking chicks stay in the nest for the first two weeks, fed a liquid, regurgitated (spit-up) diet of partially digested fish, frogs, small snakes, insects and even mice.

FLEDGLING Young birds leave the nest after the first two weeks but hang out nearby for a few more weeks, begging extra meals from Mom.

JUVENILE Lacks the black neck patch of adults. When the teens return to Minnesota in the spring from their southern wintering grounds, they are mature enough to mate and raise their own young.

Birding Tip

Covert (secret or undercover) hunting works well. The bittern wears its grass-like camouflage to hide it from the prey it is trying to catch. One of the best slow-motion actors on the marsh, a bittern moves from its "bill-to-the-sky-pretend-grass" position downward so slowly it is hard to see any movement. What is not slow is its quick dart to grab prey with its bill, shake it and swallow it headfirst.

When

American Bitterns are diurnal, active during the day and resting at night. Some bitterns call into the night.

Migration

Spring Arrival: April
Fall Departure: August–October
Long-distance migrant. Overwinters in areas with open water in the southern United States, Mexico and Central America including Panama.

Nesting

American Bitterns begin nesting in May–June in Minnesota.

Getting Around

Bitterns fly with their neck tucked in and legs hanging out behind. On land, they move in slow motion. Each leg is lifted slowly, as they spread their toes out wide before each foot touches the ground.

Where to Look

Tall, thick grasses and cattails of central and northeastern Minnesota.
· Bear Lake Area
· Agassiz Nat'l Wildlife Refuge
· Burnham Creek near Melvin
· Heron Lake
· McGregor Marsh

Year-round	Summer
Migration	Winter

Common Loon

Gavia immer

Length: 26–36 inches
Wingspan: 41–52 inches

Red eyes filter light
in deep water

Black head
and neck

Males and females molt
summer feathers to gray
winter plumage with
white below

White-striped
necklace

White breast.
Black-and-white
checkered back

Wailing means "I'm over here, fellow loons!" This can sound like the howl of a wolf or an eerie laugh.

Minnesota State Bird

Minnesota's state bird spends almost its entire life on water. With 10,000 lakes and plenty of fish, the Common Loon is at home here. Built for deep lake diving, a loon flattens its feathers to push out air and to be less buoyant. With its small, pointed wings to its sides, it plunges below the surface, paddling with webbed feet. In a short time, it strikes prey with its long, sharp-dagger bill partly open. (Loons will also stab intruders too close to their nest.) Parents train their young to catch prey by dropping fish in front of them. Chicks use their parents' backs as safety from predators and as diving platforms. How much fish does a loon family eat in a summer? Nearly one ton!

Habitat Café

Yumm . . . bring an order of fish (perch, lake trout, bullheads), minnows and aquatic insects. Common Loons are carnivorous. How do loons hold on to slippery fish? Their tongue and the roof of their mouth have sharp points that face backward like the barb on the end of a fishhook. A loons' throat expands for eating large fish.

Today's Special
frogs and crayfish

SPRING, SUMMER, FALL, WINTER MENU:
Lots of fish, a few insects

Life Cycle

NEST Loons will nest on a floating mat of plants attached to shoreline vegetation, close to the water on bare ground—even on a muskrat house. Parents add more plants to the two-foot diameter nest during incubation.

EGGS About 3½ inches long. Both the female and male incubate the clutch of 2 eggs for 28 days.

MOM! DAD! Precocial. The downy young can dive up to ten feet deep when they are ten days old. Riding on the back of Mom or Dad protects them from predators such as Northern Pike, Muskies, Snapping Turtles and Bald Eagles. The family moves farther away from motorboats and people to a nursery area, a quiet bay where the young birds have more protection from predators.

FLEDGLING Young do not fly until they are 12 weeks old. Both parents feed the chicks whole food for 2–3 months, even when the chicks can feed themselves at 6 weeks of age.

JUVENILE Juvenile loons migrate in flocks and return in the spring. They are mature enough to date, mate and raise their own young when they are at least 4 years of age.

Birding Tip

Loons need large, deep lakes of 150–500 acres with space away from people and boats, about 200 yards (the length of two soccer fields). The loon makes a tremolo call when it is upset. Use a spotting scope, binoculars or the zoom lens on your camera for a view of loons. Stay away from loon nests and report the nest location to the Minnesota DNR. Join Project Loon Watch and lend a hand to our state bird.

When

Common Loons are diurnal, active during the day and resting at night.

Migration

Spring Arrival: April–May
Fall Departure: Sept.–mid-Nov. Long-distance migrant to Atlantic coast from N. Carolina to Florida and the Gulf of Mexico. Group on large lakes (like Superior) in August and leave in September. Juveniles leave 4–6 weeks after adults.

Nesting

Common Loons begin in May–early June in Minnesota.

Getting Around

Loons can dive 250 feet and stay underwater 5 minutes. Legs positioned far back on their body propel them in the water like a torpedo. They do not walk, but scoot on land and need a very large lake for a long water take-off.

Where to Look

Deep lakes of 150–200 acres with islands or shorelines with vegetation. Central and northern Minnesota.
· Voyageurs Nat'l Park
· Superior Nat'l Forest
· Aitkin, Beltrami and Hubbard Counties

Year-round	Summer
Migration	Winter

Canada Goose

Branta canadensis

Length: 32–36 inches
Wingspan: 4–6 feet

Bill: Small saw-like points on the edges of the upper and lower mandibles help the goose grip plants and strip seeds from standing grasses

in flight

gosling

Look for their white underside and dark tail when they take off from land

Long, black neck with white throat patch

Females and males look similar, but the males are slightly larger

"Ha-roonk, ha-roonk!"

A Honking Success

Honk, honk, honk! Spring without geese overhead? The years from 1920 to the early 1960s were quiet in Minnesota. Canada Geese simply could not keep up with the draining of their wetland habitat and poaching. They were nearly gone from Minnesota when in 1955 the Twin Cities hosted their first pair of re-established Canada Geese. It was a honking success that continues today. Surprisingly, the success has led to some unexpected challenges for wildlife managers. Mated pairs of geese and their offspring come back to the same nesting place each year, causing some populations to grow very large in a few years. Wildlife managers work to balance both the needs of wildlife and people.

Habitat Café

Yumm . . . bring an order of roots, stems, leaves, fruits, berries and seeds. Canada Geese are herbivores. They also like to eat bluegrass—the kind of grass found on lakeshore lawns and golf courses.

Today's Special
field corn

SPRING, SUMMER, FALL MENU:
Aquatic plants high in protein

WINTER MENU:
Grass, agricultural crops, fruit, berries and seeds

Life Cycle

NEST Geese nest on muskrat houses, beaver lodges and floating mats of vegetation, or build their own. The female uses reeds, stems and leaves of water plants to make the bulky nest near water and lines it with her down feathers.

It's best to stay far away from nests. Females will lay their neck flat and lie motionless on the nest. Males defend the nest with gusto. They have been known to attack intruders with their strong neck, bill and wings. Spotting scopes, binoculars and a camera with a zoom lens work super for safe, close-up views of wildlife!

EGGS About 3½ inches long. The female incubates the clutch of 4–7 eggs for 28 days. Dad sits on the nest when Mom takes a break.

MOM! DAD! Precocial. The down-covered goslings are able to walk, swim, feed and dive just one day after hatching. Mom and Dad lead them to feeding areas. The goslings are fully fledged with strong flight feathers at 7–9 weeks of age.

JUVENILE Teens stay with their parents through the first year. They are mature enough at 2–5 years of age to date, mate and raise their own young.

Did You Know?

True waterfowl have toes connected by webbing to help them swim. The web is spread out to push the bird through in the water, then closed when the foot comes forward again. Webbed feet can also be used in flight to steer when landing.

When
Canada Geese are diurnal, active during the day and resting at night.

Migration
Short- to long-distant migrant to central and southern U.S. Many overwinter in Minnesota where they find open water.

Nesting
Late March–early April nesting begins in Minnesota.

Getting Around
Canada Geese can move fast for large birds, flying at speeds of 40–60 mph. Their V-formation is energy efficient, too. Flying in the slipstream of the leader, geese behind face less wind resistance and use less energy. When the lead goose tires, it changes place with another goose. Now that's teamwork.

Where to Look
Canada Geese live in Minnesota's open country with wetlands, ponds and lakeshores—even golf courses and city parks. For the best chance at spying on Canada Geese, explore city parks, state parks, area lakes, marshes and wildlife areas.
· A *Super Adaptor*

Year-round	Summer
Migration	Winter

Bald Eagle

Haliaeetus leucocephalus

Length: 31–37 inches
Wingspan: 7 feet

juvenile

fishing

Large, yellow hooked beak for tearing apart prey

Dark brown-black with a white head

Females and males look the same. Females are often larger than males.

Large yellow legs and feet with curved talons for capturing and carrying prey

White tail

"Kwit kwit kwit kwit, kee-kee-kee-kee-ker!" This is fair warning to "Stay out of my territory!"

National Symbol of the USA

Where is one of the largest breeding populations of Bald Eagles in the lower 48 states? Minnesota! In 1973, there were 115 active nests (pairs) increasing to more than 1,000 breeding pairs in 2005. The Bald Eagle's status has since changed from a state threatened species to one of special concern. At Chippewa National Forest, biologists learned what eagles need to nest successfully: tall trees, open water within one mile of the nest, food, roosting areas and not being disturbed. With more buildings being placed near the water's edge in Minnesota, eagle habitat is lost. You can help our national symbol by learning about this incredible bird and making choices that consider its needs!

Habitat Café

Yumm . . . bring an order of fish caught at the water's surface, carrion (dead meat) and water birds including gulls and ducks. Bald Eagles are carnivorous. Eagles can eat large amounts of food and store it in their crop to digest over several days.

Today's Special
ducks

SPRING, SUMMER, FALL, WINTER MENU:
Mostly fish, some birds and a few mammals and reptiles

Life Cycle

NEST Both parents build the nest, or eyrie, in the top of a large tree (cottonwood, red or white pine). The nest is a deep pile of large branches and sticks, lined with smaller twigs, grass, moss and weeds.

EGGS About 2¾ inches long. Both the female and male incubate the clutch of 2 eggs for 34–36 days.

MOM! DAD! Altricial. Covered with down for the first 5–6 weeks. Parents bring fresh food. The first chick to hatch is generally larger and may kill or starve the second, smaller chick.

NESTLING Feathers grow in at 5 weeks of age but young stay in the nest for 8–14 weeks. Before leaving the nest they practice flapping and landing skills. Half of all nest take-offs fall short, leaving the bird on the ground, vulnerable to predators. Mom and Dad come to the rescue and bring food until it can fly.

FLEDGLING Fledge at 3–4 months of age.

JUVENILE Juveniles gain their full adult plumage at five years of age. They stay with the same mate for life and remain in the same nesting territory each breeding season.

History Hangout

The National Emblem Law of 1940 made it illegal to kill any Bald Eagle in the lower 48 states. In Alaska, however, there was still a bounty of $2 for each pair of Bald Eagle feet until 1962, when this was outlawed. Today Bald Eagles are also protected under the Migratory Bird Treaty Act and the federal and Minnesota Environmental Protection Acts.

When

Bald Eagles are diurnal, active during the day and resting at night.

Migration

Spring Arrival: February–April Fall Departure: August–Dec. Partial migrant. Some stay all winter in southeast Minnesota along open waters of the Mississippi River, while others migrate to the southern United States.

Nesting

Bald Eagles begin courtship, egg-laying and incubation from late Feb. to mid-May in Minnesota.

Getting Around

Bald Eagles use their powerful, broad wings to climb in flight, and to soar and glide while searching for food and during migration.

Where to Look

Large, forested areas near lakes and rivers. Range in Minnesota has expanded south and west.
· Chippewa Nat'l Forest
· Superior Nat'l Forest
· Mississippi River, lower river corridor in winter
· Hawk Ridge, Duluth during fall migration
· Glendalough State Pk

Year-round	Summer
Migration	Winter

Trumpeter Swan

Cygnus buccinator

Height: 3½ feet
Wingspan: 7 feet

takeoff

Black bill

Males, called cobs, and females, called pens, are both white

The largest waterfowl in Minnesota

Black legs and feet

Juveniles are gray for the first few years, reaching full adult white at four years of age

The windpipe (trachea) coils through the keel of the breastbone (sternum) to make a sound like the trumpet of a French horn.

Trumpeting Toward Success

Trumpeter Swans have a touch-and-go history in Minnesota that includes the last wild nests at Heron and Everson lakes in late 1800s. By the 1880s they were gone from the state completely. In the lower 48 states, fewer than 70 of these majestic birds remained in 1935, all in a remote area of Montana. Sound the trumpet! Protective laws were put into place. Hennepin Parks hosted restoration efforts in the 1960s. Then, in 1982, the Minnesota DNR's Nongame Wildlife Program joined the effort. In the next few years, incubator suitcases carrying swan eggs traveled from Alaska to Minnesota. The resulting cygnets were raised for two years and released. Today more than 2,000 swans trumpet in Minnesota again!

Habitat Café

Yumm . . . bring an order of roots, seeds, leaves and tubers of plants that grow at the bottom and float on top of marshes and lakes. Cygnets eat insects and snails for the first 2–5 weeks after they hatch, finding their meal by the color and movement of the prey. Trumpeter Swans are herbivores.

Today's Special
wild celery

SPRING, SUMMER, FALL, WINTER MENU:
🌱 Almost entirely plant matter, with a small amount of fish and invertebrates

Life Cycle

NEST The male and female build the nest on a muskrat or beaver house or dam, on a small island, a floating mat of plants, or they may build up enough plants to make their own nesting platform.

 EGGS About 4½ inches long. The female incubates the clutch of 4–6 eggs for 34 days. Dad may help. One day before hatching, the chicks begin to peep inside the egg. Mom and Dad stay close to the nest.

MOM! DAD! Precocial. Cygnets can swim as soon as their down is dry, but they stay on the nest for a few days. They are brooded by their parents for the next three weeks until their new feathers grow in. Mom and Dad stir up snails and insects from the bottom of the marsh for the kids. Fast-growing cygnets need the extra protein found in insects and crustaceans.

JUVENILE Young swans stay with their parents through their first winter until they return in the spring to the breeding area. Teens hang out with their siblings until they are mature enough to mate and raise their own young at 4–6 years of age.

Did You Know?

The Department of Natural Resources' swan restoration effort is funded by donations to the Nongame Wildlife Check-off on state tax forms. When you see a Trumpeter Swan, it is a WILD reminder of how important the Check-off has been in helping Minnesota's wildlife. Spread the word!

When ☀️
Trumpeter Swans are diurnal, active during the day and resting at night.

Migration
In late fall, they move to wintering sites along the Otter Tail River northeast of Fergus Falls, the Mississippi River near Monticello, and farther south to Missouri, Kansas, Oklahoma and Arkansas.

Nesting
Trumpeter Swans begin nesting in May and the cygnets hatch in June in Minnesota.

Getting Around
Swans fly low over the water. They run on top of the water with their wings flapping to take off. Just after takeoff they pull their neck into an S and then straighten it out. They sleep with their head tucked under their wing.

Where to Look
Minnesota's marshes and lakes.
· Tamarac Nat'l Wildlife Refuge
· Sherburne Nat'l Wildlife Refuge
· Buffalo River State Pk
· Heron Lake
· Swan Lake
· Wild River State Pk
· Twin Lakes Wildlife Mgmt Area
· St. Croix State Pk

Year-round	Summer
Migration	Winter

Great Egret

Ardea alba

Length: 3–4 feet
Wingspan: 4 feet

aigrettes

in flight

Long, sharp yellow bill designed for spearing fish

Yellow eyes

During breeding season the top of the bill to just below the eye is apple green

A very long neck

All-white bird with black legs and feet

Females and males look the same

"Frawnk" or, "Alarm!" When you hear this call, take the hint and move farther away.

Great Egrets Escape Fashion Fad

Egrets wear beautiful, long white feathers (aigrettes) on their backs during their spring courtship season. Women in the late 1800s to the early 1900s thought wearing aigrettes in their hats would be just as gorgeous. Overhunting to pluck the fashionable feathers from the egrets nearly led to their extinction. People took action just in time to protect egrets and other nongame birds with the Migratory Bird Treaty Act of 1918. Great Egrets recovered and expanded their nesting range to include Minnesota in 1938, with the first nesting record in the state. Trek to a nearby wetland and watch Great Egrets feathered in style for the spring fashion show.

Habitat Café

Today's Special
giant water bugs

Yumm . . . bring an order of small fish, frogs, crayfish, dragonflies and whirligig beetles, tadpoles, snakes, lizards and small mammals. The long, sharp yellow bill is designed for spearing fish. Great Egrets are omnivorous.

SPRING, SUMMER, FALL, WINTER MENU:
Almost entirely fish, some reptiles, amphibians and insects

Life Cycle

NEST Both parents build the bulky, two-foot diameter nest of sticks and twigs in trees 10–30 feet above ground. Great Egrets nest on their own or in colonies with Great Blue Herons. Their feet have a special, long back toe to steady them while they perch in the nesting tree.

EGGS About 2 inches long. Both the male and female incubate the clutch of 3–4 eggs for 23–26 days.

MOM! DAD! Altricial. Both parents help feed the downy chicks.

NESTLING By the end of the first week, the chick's feathers begin to grow and are complete at 4–5 weeks of age. Like an umbrella, Mom or Dad stand over the young chicks to keep them dry when it rains!

FLEDGLING The young leave the nest to perch on nearby branches and exercise their wings at three weeks of age, but return to the nest for meals. The next week they dine out, and in yet another week or so they fly on their own.

JUVENILE Once they leave the nest, the teens go out to feeding areas during the day and return to the colony at night to roost.

Did You Know?

The Migratory Bird Act protects all migratory birds (and any part of the bird) wherever they spend their time. In addition, Minnesota laws protect all birds in the state except the Rock Pigeon, European Starling and English Sparrow. You may not collect bird feathers, nests or eggs. Draw, paint, photograph and keep notes in Journal Pages in this book for safe wildlife souvenirs.

When

Great Egrets are diurnal. They are active during the day and rest at night.

Migration

Spring Arrival: late April–May
Fall Departure: late July–October
Long-distance migrant, Central America. Great Egrets over-winter in Alabama, Louisiana, Texas and south to Honduras.

Nesting

Great Egrets nest in rookeries beginning in May–June in Minnesota.

Getting Around

Great Egrets move gracefully in flight with their neck tucked in an S shape and their black legs trailing behind! They will wade slowly during the day in water up to their belly, looking for small fish and crustaceans to eat.

Where to Look

Wetlands, rivers and shores of shallow water with open vegetation throughout Minnesota.
· Agassiz Nat'l Wildlife Refuge
· Egret Island Scientific and Natural Area
· Pelican Lake
· Lake Johanna
· Big Stone Nat'l Wildlife Refuge
· Long Lake, Willmar

Year-round	Summer
Migration	Winter

Great Blue Heron

Ardea herodias

Length: 42–52 inches
Wingspan: 4–6 feet

in flight

Feather plume

Yellow bill

Adults have a white crown
and black areas on their
wing (shoulders)

Blue-gray with
a white throat
and head

Male and female
look alike

"Rok-rok"
means
"This is my space!"

Rok-Rok, Rookeries

Great Blue Herons nest throughout Minnesota in colonies of often 100 or more birds, called rookeries. There are colonies at Pig's Eye Lake in South St. Paul, Peltier Lake in Anoka County and Lake Johanna in Pope County. Going in or near heron colonies during nesting is not a good idea. You might cause the herons to abandon their young. Besides, a heron colony is a very smelly place. Many birds together can create a lot of droppings! Heron colonies are best enjoyed at a distance. Herons may fly out to feeding areas in wetlands over 30 miles from a colony. They are much easier to find and watch as they slowly stalk shoreline shallows in search of fish and other prey.

Habitat Café

Today's Special
snakes

Yumm . . . bring an order of fish, frogs, crayfish, lizards, grasshoppers, mice and shrews. Herons grip or spear prey with their 6-inch pointed bill. Great Blue Herons are carnivorous. They eat only animal matter.

SPRING, SUMMER, FALL, WINTER MENU:
Lots of fish, with lesser amounts of insects, reptiles and amphibians

Life Cycle

NEST Hundreds of Great Blue Herons nest together in the tops of tall trees in a colony called a rookery. The nest is built of large sticks. Herons will use the same rookery for many years. The largest rookeries in Minnesota are usually on forested islands in south-eastern and central parts of the state along the Mississippi and Minnesota Rivers.

EGGS About 2½ inches long. Both the female and male incubate the clutch of 4 eggs for 28 days.

MOM! DAD! Altricial. Both help feed the young.

NESTLING The chicks stay in the nest for about 7–8 weeks.

FLEDGLING They are about the same size as their parents when they leave the nest. The parents continue to feed them for 2–3 weeks.

JUVENILE The juveniles join with others their age, feeding and preparing for migration. They have a black crown, but it takes two years to grow a full feather plume. At three years they are mature enough to nest and raise young.

Gross Factor

Parents catch, eat and partially digest fish, frogs and other small animals, and deliver the baby food by spitting it up into the chick's open beak. As chicks grow, they take the food out of the parent's beak. Finally, the parents spit the food into the nest and the older chicks fight over the juiciest pieces. Chicks ward off threats from below by leaning over the nest and spitting half-digested fish on the intruder. Gross!

When

Great Blue Herons are diurnal, feeding during the day and resting at night.

Migration

Spring Arrival: early April
Fall Departure: September
Short to long-distance migrant to the coast of southeastern U.S., Mexico and Central America as far as Panama. Migrate alone or in groups of 3–100 during the day and night.

Nesting

Pairs nest in a heron rookery during late April–June in Minnesota. Raccoons can prey heavily on nests and young, causing a population to decline in a short time.

Getting Around

Herons wade and stalk prey in shallow water, and at times, dry land. Their toes spread out as they step on the ground, leaving tracks in the mud 6–8 inches long and 4–6 inches wide. Herons fly with slow, deep, steady wing beats, legs stretched out behind, and their neck bent into a tight S-shape.

Where to Look

Great Blue Herons can be found in the shallow edges of lakes, streams, rivers and wetlands all over Minnesota.

Year-round	Summer
Migration	Winter

American White Pelican

Pelecanus erythrorhynchos

Length: 50–70 inches
Wingspan: 8–9½ feet

dinner

Bare skin around eye is yellow or orange

Enormous orange bill, 11–15 inches long, with a deep pouch for scooping food—it can hold up to three gallons of water

in flight

White with black wing tips and black along the trailing edges of wings

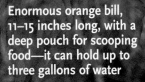

Females and males look similar

Orange legs and webbed feet

Hey, Good-looking!

What does a pelican find good-looking? Bring on the nuptial tubercles and yellow crest feathers! Spring dating and mating season calls for chic outerwear for American White Pelicans. From late winter until after the eggs are laid, the top of a pelican's bill has ridges, called nuptial tubercles, that look like a large knob. They also grow a crest of pale-yellow feathers on the back of their head. Wearing black wing tips with wide slots for soaring, a group of pelicans can turn together in the air, like a school of fish in the water. I once watched a raft of pelicans soar over Fairmont, Minnesota, flashing silvery visible and then invisible as they spiraled ever higher in a thermal. Wow!

Habitat Café

Yumm . . . bring an order of fish, fish and more fish with a side of salamanders and crayfish. Pelicans work together to increase their chances of catching fish by making a semi-circle on the water and "herding" the fish into shallow water. To eat fish, a pelican first points its beak down to drain out the water and then lifts its beak and head up—swallow! American White Pelicans are carnivorous.

SPRING, SUMMER, FALL, WINTER MENU:
Almost entirely fish, some amphibians and crustaceans

Today's Special — salamanders

Life Cycle

NEST The nest can be a low spot in the ground with no material or a mound of plants and dirt, 2–3 feet across and 15–16 inches high.

EGGS About 3½ inches long. Both the male and female incubate the clutch of 2 eggs for 29–36 days. Pelicans do not have a brood patch on their belly like most birds. Instead, they place one egg under each large, webbed orange foot for warmth!

MOM! DAD! Semi-altricial. Hatched out of the egg naked and flesh-colored (some even look green), the new chicks are covered with thick, white down within ten days.

NESTLING The chicks leave the nest at three weeks to huddle in groups. Mom and Dad visit the group to deliver food and then leave until the next mealtime.

FLEDGLING The short-legged young are ready for take-off flights by 7–8 weeks of age.

JUVENILE Teens have gray to flesh-colored bills and brown streaks on their white feathers. They migrate south in the fall and are mature enough to mate and raise young at 3–4 years of age.

Gross Factor

Young chicks eat regurgitated liquid food from the front part of their parent's throat pouch. As they grow, they reach farther back into the pouch for regurgitated food with larger pieces of fish. This transition to larger food pieces prepares them for the time when they feed themselves. Bill-smacking tasty!

When

White Pelicans are diurnal, active from sunrise to sunset.

Migration

Spring Arrival: April–May
Fall Departure: September–Nov.
Long-distance migrants. Pelicans overwinter in Alabama, Louisiana, Texas and some farther south to Honduras.

Nesting

White Pelicans nest in colonies on bare islands and sandbars. If the nest site is disturbed, they may not return the next year.

Getting Around

Their long, broad wings have widely slotted tips to soar high over land. They use rising flows of warm air, called thermals. To go into a thermal, they soar up in a spiral of rising warm air and then drift down to the bottom of the next thermal. Soaring saves energy on long trips.

Where to Look

White Pelicans like large lakes and rivers.
· Leech Lake
· Heron Lake
· Minnesota Lake
· Marsh Lake
· Lake of the Woods
· Pigeon Lake

Year-round	Summer
Migration	Winter

YOU MIGHT INCLUDE:
- size, shape, field marks
- type of bill and feet
- shape of wings and tail
- feather color and pattern

The Robin I saw on 5/20/07 was 9 inches long and robin shaped. It had a medium sized bill and I couldn't see its feet. It was standing in the grass. It was orange on the front and dark brown on the back and sides. Tail also was brown. It didn't make any noise or singing and was all by itself. It was poking the ground with its beak. It was probably hungry and looking for worms. I saw a robin nest yesterday.

Sample Journal Entry

OTHER NOTES YOU MAY WANT TO INCLUDE:
- Date, time and habitat
- What the bird was doing (behavior)
- Song/call
- Alone, pair or group of birds
- Flight pattern
- Other signs like tracks, scat (droppings), nests, eggs, wood chips, wing marks in snow, ice crystals from a snow burrow

Let's start a journal to record your adventures as an outdoor detective!

SEE HOW MANY BIRDS YOU CAN FIND

Let's start a journal to record your adventures as an outdoor detective!

SEE HOW MANY BIRDS YOU CAN FIND

Glossary

Brainy Bird Words and Their Meanings

adaptation A physical feature, behavior or trait that a bird has developed to help it take full advantage of its habitat. American Robins are found all over Minnesota because they have adapted to a variety of habitats for shelter, nesting and raising their young. They have also adapted to eating a variety of foods. A robin's diet includes worms, insects, seeds, berries and fruits. These meals can be found in rural, city or suburban habitats around the state.

altricial Baby birds that hatch from the egg helpless. They are naked, unable to see, walk, hop, fly or feed themselves, and need to be cared for by one or both parents.

anting Some birds, such as the Blue Jay, will place ants between their skin and their feathers with their beak. At times, some birds actually stand on an anthill and allow the ants to crawl up into their feathers!

binomial nomenclature A system of classifying and giving scientific names to plants and animals based on similar identifying characteristics. It is used to group birds together by which body characteristics they have in common. Scientific names are in Latin and remain the same all over the world. The scientific name for the American Robin is *Turdus migratorius*.

boreal migrant Birds that breed in Canada, but come south into Minnesota during some years when their northern food supply is scarce.

bristle feathers Stiff, hair-like feathers made up of a firm central shaft (rachis). They usually grow near the eyes, nostrils and beak opening. Bristle feathers may protect the eyes from insects and debris, or help the bird funnel food into its mouth.

brood patch A bare spot on the chest or belly of a parent bird that is used to incubate eggs. The feathers in this area either fall off or are plucked out. Blood vessels next to the brood patch help keep the eggs warm.

camouflage A bird's shape, or the color and pattern of its feathers (plumage), that helps it hide from predators or prey. The American Woodcock's plumage is similar in color and pattern to the brown leaves of the deciduous forest where it lives.

coniferous trees Trees that bear their seeds in a cone. Minnesota's coniferous trees include red pine, white pine, jack pine, balsam fir, red cedar, white cedar, black spruce, white spruce and tamarack.

contour feathers These feathers overlap each other to give birds a streamlined body shape (a contour) for less friction. This helps birds fly faster through the air and dive faster in the water. Contour feathers are found on the body, wings and tail. They have a central shaft (rachis) with vanes on each side. Attached to the vanes are barbs. On each side of the barbs are small barbules that make a "zipper" to hold the feather barbs together. When the barbs unzip, the bird uses its beak to zip them back together while preening.

courtship behavior The things that a bird does to attract a mate. Some birds stomp the ground and turn in circles in a courtship dance. Others perform amazing aerial dances, and some drum on hollow trees. Courtship is the "dating" behavior of birds.

crepuscular Active during the twilight hours, which include the hours of dawn just before the sun rises, and dusk just after the sun sets. Crepuscular birds are active during the time between day and night when the faint light of sunrise and sunset provides them with protection from predators. American Woodcocks are mostly crepuscular.

deciduous forest A forest of trees that lose their all of their leaves each year. In Minnesota, maples, oaks, elm, ash, fruit trees and cottonwoods are examples of deciduous trees.

diurnal Active during the daytime, or the hours that the sun is up. Diurnal birds feed, build their nests and preen during the day. American Robins are diurnal birds.

down feathers These feathers do not "zip" together like contour feathers, but stay fluffy. The air spaces hold the bird's body heat close like a warm blanket. Young birds often have down first to keep their small bodies warm until their contour and other body feathers grow in. Adult birds' down feathers are located under their contour feathers.

egg-tooth A newly hatched chick has an egg-tooth. This small, sharp projection on its upper mandible (bill) helps it to chip through the egg's shell during hatching. The egg-tooth is no longer needed after hatching and soon falls off.

field marks Each bird species has physical features that make it unique (one of a kind). These unique features can help you to identify it. Field marks include feather color, feather pattern, a bird's basic body shape and size. Other field marks include the shape and size of the bird's bill, feet, wings and tail. An eye-ring (which gives the bird the appearance of wearing a pair of glasses) or a crest on the top of its head are also field marks.

fledgling Young birds that have just learned to fly on their own and have left the family nest are called fledglings. To fledge is to be fully feathered and be able to sustain flight.

filoplume feather Delicate, hair-like feathers that help a bird adjust the position of its contour feathers for better flight. Filoplume feathers are scattered over a bird's body. They are sensitive enough to move with the slightest breeze, and send information to nerve cells at their bases.

foraging Gathering food.

game wildlife Birds and other wildlife that can be legally hunted under Minnesota law during designated times of the year. Hunting seasons and limits are specific to each species.

glean To collect or pick up, often referring to gathering food. When a bird picks insect larvae from cracks in tree bark, or spilled grain from a harvested farm field, it is said to be "gleaning."

habitat The place where a bird lives. For a Mallard, home is a shallow lake or wetland habitat where it can reach for the plants and animals on the lake or wetland bottom with its long neck and bill. For a Pileated Woodpecker, home is in a forest habitat with trees big enough for it to make large nesting and roosting holes.

hawking The act of catching insects on the wing in short, quick flights.

juvenile A young bird that has grown to be independent of its parents (it can fly and find food, water and shelter on its own) but is not yet mature enough to breed. Many smaller birds pass through this stage in their first year; larger birds can remain a juvenile for four or five years. They are the adolescents and teenagers of the bird world.

lift This is what allows a bird to defy gravity and get off the ground. Lift is made by the force of the air pressure underneath the wings, which is greater than the air pressure above the wings, and results in a raising force. The shape of a bird's wings is what makes this work. The top side of the wing is convex (curved), and the bottom is flatter. The air rushing past the wing is divided in two flows: one over the top of the wing and the other past the bottom of the wing. The top air moves faster. This causes the air beneath the wing to go slower and increases the air pressure under the wing—the bird is lifted off the ground. The Swiss scientist Daniel Bernoulli (1700–1782) discovered this principle of flight, which is now called Bernoulli's Principle.

migration The seasonal movement of birds or animals from one region to another. Purple Martins migrate to wintering grounds in South America in early September and return to Minnesota the following spring to nest and raise their young.

molt When a bird sheds its old feathers and grows in new ones to replace them.

navigation How a bird finds its way, such as during migration.

neotropical migrant A bird that breeds in Minnesota, but migrates to wintering areas in Central and South America. Includes both mid-distance Central American and long-distance South American migrants.

nocturnal Active during the night. Birds that are nocturnal are active feeding, nest building and preening during the night. Great Horned Owls are nocturnal birds.

nongame wildlife Birds and animals protected by state or national laws from trapping and hunting. Most birds in this book are nongame birds. There is no designated time or "season" to legally hunt them. Game birds, however, can be legally hunted.

ornithology The study of birds. The segment "ology" in a word means the study of, and "ornith" is associated with birds. An ornithologist is a scientist who studies birds.

overwinter To spend the winter. Many Canada Geese overwinter in Minnesota.

permanent resident Birds that breed and remain in Minnesota all year. Black-capped Chickadees and Blue Jays are permanent residents in Minnesota.

phenology The study of the changing seasons.

plumage A bird's plumage refers to all of its feathers together.

prairie Land covered with native grasses and flowering plants with few to no trees. In Minnesota, the western quarter of the state was once covered by prairie, described by Native Americans and pioneers alike as an ocean of grass. Today, only small remnants of the original prairie remain in publicly and privately owned areas. Plants and animals that have adapted over tens of thousands of years to the conditions of the prairie habitat can be found on these unique areas of Minnesota.

precocial Chicks that hatch able to see, walk, hop or fly and feed themselves. They need only limited care by one or both parents. The role of the parents in precocial birds is usually to lead the young to food, offer protection from predators, and provide brooding in weather and temperature extremes. The young of many ground-nesting birds such as the Killdeer and Canada Goose are precocial.

predator A bird or animal that captures other living creatures to eat. A Cooper's Hawk is a predator of small mammals that it catches for lunch.

preening When a bird arranges, cleans, fluffs and straightens its feathers.

prey A bird or animal that is captured and eaten by a predator. The small mammals captured for lunch by a Cooper's Hawk are considered its prey.

semiplume feather A combination of a contour feather and a down feather. It has a stiff shaft and soft down veins that serve as extra insulation to keep a bird warm.

short distance migrant A bird that breeds in Minnesota but winters just far enough south to avoid extreme temperatures and snowfall.

super adaptor A bird that is able to live in a variety of habitats.

syrinx The vocal organ of a bird similar to the larynx (voice box) in humans. Birds use the syrinx to call and sing.

territory A bird's territory is the space that it defends from other birds (and sometimes mammals such as squirrels) for feeding, courtship, nesting and raising its young.

undulating To move in waves.

uropygium gland A gland located above a bird's tail that holds oil. The bird squeezes the gland with its bill to get the oil and then spreads the oil onto its feathers for waterproofing.

warm-blooded All birds are warm-blooded. They can keep a constant body temperature no matter how hot or cold the weather. Mammals like you are also warm-blooded. Reptiles and amphibians are cold-blooded. They take on the temperature of their surroundings.

webbed feet When a bird's toes are connected to one another by thick skin, the bird is said to have webbed feet. Mallards, Canada Geese and Blue-winged Teals have webbed feet that help them paddle through the water.

wetlands Areas of land that hold water in their soils or are covered with water during all or part of the year. Wetlands can be found separate from other bodies of water, or associated with the shallow edges of a river or lake. Bogs are a special kind of wetland that are very acidic and have a buildup of peat. Plants and animals living in wetland habitats have special adaptations to make the most of the watery conditions.

Do the Math Answer Key

Do the math on your own first and then check if you have figured the answer correctly. If you have not, review the equations in this answer key to find where you worked the math differently. Use your brain power, you can do it!

Ruby-throated Hummingbird

This solution is based on the weight of a 100 pound person. Put your weight in and rework the problem.

Step #1:   Change the percent to a decimal

$$30\% = .30. = .30$$

Step #2:   .30 X 100 pounds of body weight = 30 pounds increase in body weight

Ruffed Grouse

-27° at the snow's surface + 24° seven inches under the snow = 51 degrees of difference between the temperature at the surface of the snow and the temperature seven inches under the snow. Wow, snow is an efficient insulator!

-27°	0°	+24°

Great Gray Owl

Great Gray Owl invasions occurred in the following years in Minnesota. Can you find a pattern?

| 1989 | 1993 | 1997 | 2001 | 2005 |

1989 + 4 = 1993	or	1993 − 1989 = 4 years
1993 + 4 = 1997	or	1997 − 1993 = 4 years
1997 + 4 = 2001	or	2001 − 1997 = 4 years
2001 + 4 = 2005	or	2005 − 2001 = 4 years
2005 + 4 = 2009	or	2009 − 2005 = 4 years

The next invasion of Great Gray Owls into Minnesota is predicted to be in 2009.

American Robin

14 feet of earthworms per day x 7 days = A robin can eat 98 feet of earthworms in one week! Line up 98 feet of gummy worms, pipe cleaners or string on your sidewalk or driveway to see this amazing feat for yourself!

Cooper's Hawk

66 prey X 3 chicks = 198 prey needed to feed 3 young hawks for six weeks

66 prey X 4 chicks = 264 prey needed to feed 4 young hawks for six weeks

66 prey X 5 chicks = 330 prey needed to feed 5 young hawks for six weeks

Pileated Woodpecker

15 drumbeats per series X 5 times in a row X 10 minutes = 750 drumbeats in just ten minutes!

Red-winged Blackbird

This solution is based on a birth weight of 8 pounds. Place your birth weight in and rework the problem.

8 pounds birth weight x 10 days = A weight gain of 80 pounds in just 10 days!

Yellow-headed Blackbird

300,000 seeds in one cattail X 80,000 cattail heads per acre = 2,400,000 cattail seeds parachuting through the air!

Now you know why there are cattails growing in shallow wet areas all over Minnesota!

Use the Space Below to Work the Numbers

Great Places to Learn More About Birds

Share this chart and map with your family and friends to find places near you to visit and learn more about Minnesota's amazing birds and the habitats they live in.

Map #	Center Name	City	Phone Number	Web or Email Address
1	Agassiz Environmental Learning Center (ELC)	Fertile	218-945-3129	www.fertilebeltrami.k12.mn.us/Agassiz/Agassiz_files/1page.htm
2	Audubon Center of the North Woods	Sandstone	1-888-404-7743	www.audubon-center.com
3	Baker Near-Wilderness Reserve	Maple Plain	763-694-7856	www.threeriversparkdistrict.org
4	Bell Museum of Natural History	Minneapolis	612-624-7083	www.bellmuseum.org
5	Bonanza Educational Center	Clinton	320-839-3118	www.dnr.state.mn.us/state_parks/big_stone_lake/index.html
6	Boulder Lake	Duluth	218-721-3731	www.nrri.umn.edu/boulder
7	Courage ELC, Camp Courage	Maple Lake	320-963-3121	
8	Deep Portage Conservation Reserve	Hackensack	218-682-2325	www.deep-portage.org
9	Dodge Nature Center	St. Paul	651-455-4531	www.dodgenaturecenter.org
10	Eagle Bluff ELC	Lanesboro	888-800-9558	www.eagle-bluff.org
11	Eastman Nature Center	Dayton	763-694-7700	www.threeriversparkdistrict.org
12	Farm by the Lake Nature Center	Bagley	218-694-2840	fbtl@bagley.polaristel.net
13	Foley Nature Center	Pine River	218-543-6161	www.campfoley.com
14	French Regional Park	Plymouth	763-559-7932	www.ci.orono.MN.us/french_regional_park.htm
15	Harriet Alexander Nature Center	Roseville	651-765-4262	www.ci.roseville.mn.us/parks/facilities/hanc
16	Hartley Nature Center	Duluth	218-724-6735	www.hartleynature.org
17	Headwaters Science Center	Bemidji	218-444-4472	www.hscbemidji.org
18	Heritage Park Nature Center	St Cloud	320-255-7255	
19	Hormel Nature Center	Austin	507-437-7519	www.ci.austin.mn.us/Parkandrec/outdoor.html
20	Lake Minnetonka Visitor Center	Minnetrista	952-474-4822	www.threeriversparkdistrict.org/parks/park.cfm?pid=13
21	Laurentian Environmental Center	Britt	888-749-1288	www.laurentiancenter.com
22	Lee & Rose Warner Nature Center	Marine on St. Croix	651-433-2427	www.smm.org/warnernaturecenter/
23	Lawndale ELC	Herman	320-677-2203	
24	Long Lake Conservation Center	Palisade	800-450-5522	www.llcc.org
25	Lowry Nature Center	Victoria	763-469-7650	www.threeriversparkdistrict.org
26	Minnesota Landscape Arboretum	Chaska	952-443-1400	www.arboretum.umn.edu
27	Mississippi Headwaters Hostel, Itasca SP	Lake Itasca	218-266-3415	www.dnr.state.mn.us/state_parks/itasca/index.html
28	MSU Regional Science Center	Moorhead	218-477-2904	www.mnstate.edu/regsci/
29	National Eagle Center	Wabasha	877-332-4537	www.nationaleaglecenter.org
30	Ney ELC	Henderson	507-248-3474	www.neycenter.org/
31	Oxbow Nature Center	Byron	507-775-2451	www.oxbowpark.com
32	Paul Bunyan Nature Learning Center	Brainerd	218-829-9620	www.pbnlc.net
33	Pezuta Zizi Cultural & ELC	Granite Falls	320-564-4777	
34	Pipestone National Monument	Pipestone	507-825-5464	www.nps.gov/pipe/
35	Prairie Ecology Bus Center	Lakefield	507-662-5064	www.ecologybus.org
36	Prairie Woods ELC	Spicer	320-354-5894	www.prairiewoodselc.org
37	Prairie Wetlands Learning Center	Fergus Falls	218-736-0938	www.fws.gov/midwest/pwlc

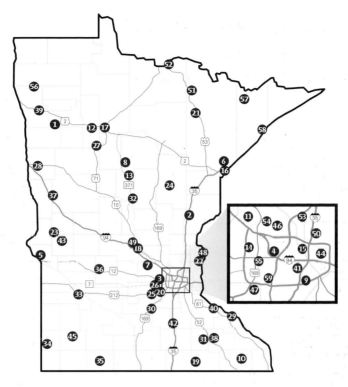

Map #	Center Name	City	Phone Number	Web Address
38	Quarry Hill Nature Center	Rochester	507-281-6114	www.qhnc.org/
39	Red River Valley Natural History Center	Crookston	218-281-8129	www.maes.umn.edu/components/rocnw
40	Red Wing ELC	Red Wing	651-388-7339	www.redwingelc.org
41	Richardson Nature Center	Bloomington	763-694-7676	www.threeriversparkdistrict.org
42	River Bend Nature Center	Faribault	507-332-7151	www.rbnc.org
43	Scandia Woods Environmental Learning Lab	Morris	320-589-2379	
44	Science Museum of Minnesota	St. Paul	800-221-9444	www.smm.org
45	Shetek ELC	Slayton	507-763-3567	
46	Springbrook Nature Center	Fridley	763-572-3588	www.springbrooknaturecenter.org
47	Staring Lake Outdoor Center	Eden Prairie	952-949-8479	www.edenprairie.org
48	St. Croix National Scenic Riverway	St. Croix Falls	715-483-3284	www.nps.gov/sacn/
49	St. John's Arboretum, St. John's University	Collegeville	320-363-3126	www.csbsju.edu/arboretum
50	Tamarack Nature Center	White Bear Lake	651-407-5350	www.co.ramsey.mn.us/parks/tamarack
51	Vince Shute Wildlife Sanctuary	Orr	218-757-0172	www.americanbear.org
52	Voyageurs National Park	International Falls	218-283-9821	www.nps.gov/voya
53	Wargo Nature Center	Lino Lakes	651-429-8007	www.anokacountyparks.com
54	West Coon Rapids Dam Visitors Center	Brooklyn Park	763-694-7790	www.threeriversparkdistrict.org
55	Westwood Hills ELC	St. Louis Park	952-924-2544	www.stlouispark.org
56	Wetlands, Pines and Prairie Audubon Sanctuary	Warren	218-745-5663	www.wiktel.net
57	Widjiwagan-North Woods ELC	Ely	218-365-2117	
58	Wolf Ridge ELC	Finland	800-523-2733 (MN & WI)	www.wolf-ridge.org
59	Wood Lake Nature Center	Richfield	612-861-9365	www.woodlakenaturecenter.org

Bird Species by Taxonomic Order

This taxonomic list draws from the common Linnean system, which classifies birds and other living things by their morphological (physical) features. It was developed over two hundred years ago by Carl Linnaeus, a Swedish naturalist. Learn more about scientific names on page 13, in "Binomial Nomenclature."

ANSERIFORMES: DUCKS, GEESE, SWANS, WATERFOWL
- Canada Goose
- Trumpeter Swan
- Wood Duck
- Mallard
- Blue-winged Teal
- Northern Shoveler

GALLIFORMES: CHICKENS, QUAIL, TURKEYS, PHEASANTS
- Ring-necked Pheasant
- Ruffed Grouse
- Spruce Grouse
- Greater Prairie-Chicken
- Wild Turkey

GAVIFORMES: LOONS
- Common Loon

PODICIPEDIFORMES: GREBES
- Pied-billed Grebe

PELECANIFORMES: PELICANS
- American White Pelican

CICONIIFORMES: HERONS, BITTERNS
- American Bittern
- Great Blue Heron
- Great Egret

FALCONIFORMES: EAGLES, HAWKS, FALCONS
- Bald Eagle
- Northern Harrier
- Cooper's Hawk
- Red-tailed Hawk
- American Kestrel

GRUIFORMES: CRANES, COOTS, RAILS
- American Coot

CHARADRIIFORMES: SHOREBIRDS, GULLS, TERNS, PLOVERS, SANDPIPERS
- Killdeer
- Spotted Sandpiper
- American Woodcock
- Ring-billed Gull

COLUMBIFORMES: DOVES, PIGEONS
- Mourning Dove

STRIGIFORMES: OWLS
- Great Horned Owl
- Snowy Owl
- Burrowing Owl
- Barred Owl
- Great Gray Owl

APODIFORMES: HUMMINGBIRDS
- Ruby-throated Hummingbird

CORACIIFORMES: KINGFISHERS
- Belted Kingfisher

PICIFORMES: WOODPECKERS
- Downy Woodpecker
- Pileated Woodpecker

PASSIFORMES: PERCHING BIRDS, SONGBIRDS
- Eastern Kingbird
- Gray Jay
- Blue Jay
- Horned Lark
- Purple Martin
- Black-capped Chickadee
- Boreal Chickadee
- Red-breasted Nuthatch
- White-breasted Nuthatch
- Brown Creeper
- House Wren
- Marsh Wren
- Ruby-crowned Kinglet
- Eastern Bluebird
- American Robin
- Brown Thrasher
- Ovenbird
- Scarlet Tanager
- Grasshopper Sparrow
- White-throated Sparrow
- Dark-eyed Junco
- Northern Cardinal
- Indigo Bunting
- Dickcissel
- Bobolink
- Red-winged Blackbird
- Western Meadowlark
- Yellow-headed Blackbird
- Baltimore Oriole
- Purple Finch
- American Goldfinch
- Evening Grosbeak

This order follows the most recent version accepted by the American Ornithologists' Union.